Air Fryer Co for Beginners

The First <u>365 Days of Recipes Full-Colored</u> Air Fryer Book with <u>Beautiful Images</u>. Quick & Easy Everyday Ideas to Fry, Grill, Roast, and Bake.

<u>Sara Dean</u>

interim quality. Trademarks that are mentioned are done without written consent and can in no way be considered an endorsement from the trademark holder.

Table of Contents

Chapter 3: Bread and Pizza 31

Chapter 4: Vegetables and Vegetarian35

Chapter 5: Poultry Recipes 44

Chapter 6: Red Meat 52

Introduction

Air fryers have started to become popular, due to the fact that you can avoid many of the unhealthy aspects of modern cooking. But what is an air fryer exactly, and how on earth does it work?

Air fryers are basically an upgraded, enhanced countertop oven, but they became popular for one particular reason. In fact, many of the manufacturers, such as Philips, market this machine solely based on the claim that the air fryers accurately mimic deep-frying, which, although extremely unhealthy, is still very popular in this day and age (as it is, in my opinion, one of the most delicious ways to eat food).

Air fryers work with the use of a fan and a heating mechanism. You place the food you want cooked in a basket or on the rack, turn on the machine, and the air fryer distributes oven-temperature hot air around your food. It provides consistent, pervasive heat evenly to all the food within. This heat circulation achieves the crispy taste and texture that is so tantalizing in deep fried foods, but without the unhealthy and dangerous oil! Both have been replaced by this miracle machine with hot air and a fan.

Advantages to Using an Air Fryer

I may have already slipped in a few of the advantages to using an air fryer, but now let's expand a little more on everything an air fryer can do for you. After all, no investment should be made unless it's absolutely worthwhile.

And in truth, the air fryer is very worthwhile. I cannot begin to tell you how the advantages start piling up; this is not just another average appliance that everyone is getting because of a simple trend. People are getting air fryers because of their incredible, numerous, multifaceted benefits.

There are, however, a few notable advantages of using an air fryer, which I'll list below. If you don't know anything else about air fryers, I hope that these will convince you of their worth.

Healthier Cooking

This is perhaps the top benefit that comes with air frying. In a society that really struggles with healthy cooking, we can use all the help we can get. Luckily, air fryers make it easy, all while maintaining many of the factors that make unhealthy food delicious!
Air fryers use very little oil, which is one of the best ways to replace those unhealthy fried foods, like fried chicken, potatoes, and so many others. If you are like me (a lover of deep fried foods) then this is the answer to your dilemma of healthy eating while still enjoying the crispy taste of food!

Do keep in mind that you still need to spray fried foods, such as fish, with a touch of oil to make sure it does get evenly crispy. All in all, however, there is no denying the amount of oils is a whole lot less.

This singular change makes all the difference in the world. Healthy eating has never been easier, as you'll get the same crispy and flavorsome results, with minimal amounts of added oils. You'll even be able to "fry" foods you never were able to before—the possibilities are endless!

Safer and Easier

Nothing scares me more than a hot pot of oil. It is an accident waiting to happen, and getting struck with burning oil splatters is no joke! But this, and its corresponding injuries, is often the price to pay for deep fried foods.

Air fryers are also user-friendly, and this makes a huge difference. You don't have to feel like you are studying for a degree when working with an air fryer. Making dinner is far less complicated in an air fryer than many of the traditional methods of cooking. For some meals—unless you choose one of the more complex recipes I'll share later—you can even revert to placing a small piece of meat (even if it happens to be frozen!) into the basket and select the cooking settings.

The simplicity of the air fryer is its beauty. You will save countless time and unnecessary frustrations, and still make delicious food!

Faster Than Cooking in the Oven

Once you buy an air fryer and set it to heat for the first time, you won't know what hit you! The average normal oven needs about 10 minutes to preheat. Due to the air fryer's smaller size and innovative design, it will be ready to go in no time!

It's even faster during the actual cooking. With the circulation that allows your food to be cooked crisp and even, it cuts a whole lot of cooking time out of the equation. This is amazing, especially in this day and age where technology, work, friends, family, and even pets are constantly demanding our attention.

Just imagine! You could set your food in the air fryer, and (with some recipes) it will be ready to eat in less than 20 minutes!

Saves Space

If you are someone living in a small apartment, or a student accommodation, then an air fryer is perfect for you. Air fryers are much smaller in comparison to a conventional oven and you can easily make use of this air fryer in 1 cubic foot of your kitchen.

You can even pack your air fryer away after use if need be, but the majority of people choose to keep it out on the counter. But it's nice to have the option to move your air fryer around if space becomes an issue.

Low Operating Costs

Considering how much cooking oil costs these days and the amount you need to use, you will soon be cutting costs in making deep fried foods. All an air fryer uses is a small amount of oil and some of the electricity to power up the air fryer, about the same amount that a countertop oven would.

Not only will you be cutting out the massive oil costs, which will save money, you will likely also save money by ordering out less, as you'll be able to replicate your favorite foods quickly and easily at home!

No Oil Smell

In reality, smelling like the food you just ate is not impressive, regardless of how delicious the food may be. This is what often happens, however, when people enjoy deep fried foods.

When deep frying foods, it also causes the whole house to smell, and as the oil splatters around, it can leave a massive mess. The oil can even harden on the walls, causing grime to build up into a nasty concentration of dirt and grease.

With less cooking oil, air fryers don't have any of those oil smells and keeps the space cleaner around you, as all the oils, smells, and actual cooking are contained within the machine.

Preserves Nutrients

When you are cooking your food in an air fryer, it actually protects a lot of the food from losing all its moisture. This means that with the use of a little oil, as well as circulation with hot air, it can allow your food to keep most of its nutrients which is excellent for you!

If you want to cook healthy foods with the purpose of maintaining as many nutrients as possible, then an air fryer is perfect for you!

Easier to Clean

Cleaning is perhaps the bane of my existence, especially after cooking and having a long day. This can really take away a lot of the pleasure of making yourself a great meal. But an air fryer lightens the burden by being easy to clean!

Consistent cleaning after using it (much like any pot or pan) can allow for easier and simpler living. You just need some soapy water and a non-scratch sponge to clean both the exterior and the interior of your air fryer. Some air fryers are even dishwasher-safe!

Great Flavour

The flavor of air fryer "fried" foods is nearly identical to traditional frying, and the texture is exact. You can cook a lot of those great frozen foods, such as onion rings or french fries, and still achieve that crunchy effect. This certainly can help you turn to healthier foods, especially if your goal is for healthy but quality meals.

The air fryer helps to cook your food to perfect crispness, instead of the soggy mess that happens when you try alternative methods of cooking foods that are meant to be deep fried (like chicken tenders). No one really enjoys mushy food. The air fryer keeps that desired element while remaining healthy.

All you will really need is just some cooking oil sprayed outside of your food to end up with a cooked interior and a crunchy exterior. So no worries! You still can eat your foods with a crunch and a healthier result!

Versatile

Unlike rice cookers meant just for rice, or bread makers meant just for bread, you will find that an air fryer leaves a lot of room to be both versatile and healthier. You can cook almost anything you would like in the air fryer (as long as it fits). From spaghetti squash, to desserts, even to fried chicken!
You will probably never run out of air frying options!

Various Types of Air Fryers and How to Choose the One for You

There isn't one standardized choice of air fryers, which means you are far more likely to find an air fryer that really suits your particular needs. Whether it be size or price, you have a wider variety of choices than what normally comes with conventional ovens.
So what are the key aspects that you need to take into consideration when getting yourself a nice air fryer? Let's begin:

- **Dimensions:** Obviously they come in different sizes, and despite saving space, some can still be bulky. When thinking about your countertop, you do want to consider its size and dimensions. You don't want to play a game of tilt with your air fryer, nor have it taken up all the extra space you have!

- **Safety Features:** You may want to check that it has an auto shutoff, as it is certainly a desirable feature. Air fryers can get very hot during use, and an auto-shutoff can save you a lot of stress and fire emergencies. Furthermore, having a cool exterior can prevent potential red and burnt hands. So do yourself a favor and make sure they have all these elements at hand.

- **Reviews:** Naturally, this is the best thing to check out. Considering that the businesses rarely give out all the information, you will certainly find it out when people leave reviews. The customer hides nothing, and if they are unhappy, they make sure everyone else knows about it. However, if people are very happy, many of them will also note it in the reviews, and it is best to target the air fryers that tend to have the high reviews.

Two Common Differences

Beyond those functional differences, there are two mainstream designs of air fryers: basket air fryers and oven air fryers. Each has very unique and distinguished features in which to enjoy. Let us take a look at the differences between the two:

Basket Air Fryers

Basket fryers are known to need less space than oven air fryers, which is very practical if you have limited space. Not only does it save space, but it also saves time, as the food is quickly heated up (without unnecessarily heating up the kitchen). Unlike an oven air fryer, and the larger traditional oven, it only takes about 1-2 minutes for the basket air fryer to heat up, and it is quite easy to place the foods inside of the basket.

The cons are, for one, that it does make a lot more noise than the oven air fryer. You also will not be able to watch the food as it cooks, which can increase the chances of burnt food if you are not careful. Also, a basket air fryer may not be the best if you need to cook a lot of food, as it is limited in capacity. This means that batch cooking may be required if you need a large amount of food.

This makes a basket air fryer ideal if you have a limited budget, don't need to cook a huge amount of food, and have limited free time. They are quick, small, and convenient, especially perfect for people who are students or single working professionals, and maybe even you!

Oven Air Fryers

Oven air fryers, in contrast, have a larger capacity, which means you can cook a lot more food at the same time. They also have multiple functions for cooking and cut down on the noise than the basket air fryer. You will also be able to move the food closer or even further away from the heating element. There is a lot more flexibility involved in the use of an oven air fryer. Best of all, you can place parts of the oven air fryer into the dishwasher to be washed (thus cutting down the cleaning process, if you happen to have a dishwasher).

But, do be aware that it takes up more counter space, and takes a larger initial bite out of your wallet. It may also heat up the kitchen more, and if you are in fashion and aesthetic design, it might be disappointing to find out the colors and themes are more limited than basket air fryers.

These are the two main common types of air fryers; however, there are new types of air fryers that are coming to light for you to use and enjoy, most notably, the paddle-type air fryer. This version has a paddle that moves through the basket of your air fryer in order to help circulate hot air in between each piece of food.

This saves you the effort of pulling your food out at a specific time and shaking or stirring it. These can also be noisy, and heat up the space, and are not small and convenient; however, if you are someone looking for convenience, then this is the air fryer to go for.

Accessory Tools for Air Fryer Cooking

I love how air fryers save time, so I've compiled a list of my favorite time-saving tools that I often use when meal prepping with my air fryer. Anything to help make your life easier and healthier should certainly be considered, and what better way to help than by adding some accessories to your air fryer inventory?

Mandoline

Preparation is always needed before jumping into air frying, and getting yourself the mandoline slicer is the perfect tool to slice online rings, pickles, or even the best and crunchiest chips. You can select the thickness or thinness, depending on what the recipe needs and says, so you will always be able to get the perfect crispness.

Grill Pan

This is simply a pan created with a perforated surface. With this tool, you can both grill and sear foods like fish or even vegetables inside your air fryer. They are also commonly non-stick, which really helps your overall cleanup.

However, before you purchase a grill pan, make sure the air fryer model you have does support the grill pan. The last thing you want is to find that your grill pan just does not fit inside your air fryer.

Heat Resistant Tongs

There is no denying how hot an air fryer can get inside, and unless you are a superhero, you will need some help maneuvering in foods in and outside of the basket if need be. Using heat-resistant tongs can really make your life infinitely easier by keeping your foods, and your hands, safe. They are affordable, and really useful to allow for an even cooking process.

Air Fryer Liners

If you'd like to further decrease your clean-up time, then this is for you! These liners are both non-stick and non-toxic, making this a classic little investment for you to consider. They prevent the food from sticking to your air fryer and help in the process of keeping your little machine clean. You will not have to worry about burnt foods inside your fryer again!

Air Fryer Rack

This adds a little bit more versatility as you can really take advantage of the surface cooking. With a rack, you ensure that heat is evenly distributed to all 360 degrees of your food. They are very safe and easy to use, and they increase the number of dishes you can cook at the same time

Baking Pans

With an air fryer, you can even bake! You just need the right equipment, such as a barrel or round pan. With this you can even bake pizza, bread, muffins, and more. Imagine telling people you baked your own cake with an air fryer!

Silicone Baking Cups

From egg bites to muffins, these are individual cups you can use in order to help compensate for the smaller space within an air fryer. The silicone material is heat-resistant, and allows for easier release of the contents, which spares you a lot of time cleaning. If you are a fan of baking, then this is a must have.

Oil Sprayer

Naturally, one of the top benefits is needing much less oil when cooking with an air fryer, but it does not necessarily mean that you can cook with no oil at all. An oil sprayer is the key to getting the food you want to that nice golden-brown. You can use any oil that you like to use when cooking; all you need is a little spritz before you close the machine, and you are set!

Thermapen

Having the right cooking time is very important, but temperature also counts for a lot, and this is a nice little accessory to add to your collection. Having an instant-read thermometer can ensure all the food you have is cooked (and evenly so). If you are not completely certain at what temperatures food should be, you can always check out the various different guides.

How To Clean An Air Fryer

As mentioned before, an air fryer is really easy to clean, but that doesn't mean you'll never need to clean it! Also, please remember that the cleanliness of your machine depends on how often you use it, and what you use it for.

It is recommended that you clean your air fryer after every use. As tempting as it may be to skip a day, it really is not worth it over the long run.

And that is the first step that comes with cleaning an air fryer:

- Do not delay the cleaning. Simply don't. Allowing crumbs or random bits of food to harden overnight can turn an easy task into a nightmare of a chore. If you do happen to air-fry foods that come with a form of sticky sauce, then the warmer they are, the easier again they will be to clean and remove.

- Unplug the machine, and use warm and soapy water to properly remove the dirt and components. You do not want anything abrasive in there. If there is food that gets stuck, try soaking it until it is soft enough to remove.

- If there is any food that happens to be stuck on the grate or in the basket, then you should consider gently using a toothpick or even a wooden skewer to scrape it off, in order to be thorough with your cleaning process.

- Remember to wipe the inside with a damp, soapy cloth, and remember to remove both the drawer and the basket.

- Finally, wipe the outside of your air fryer with a damp cloth or a sponge.

If there are any odors that seem to be stuck to your air fryer after cooking a strong food, even after you have cleaned it, then you can consider using a product called NewAir.

Just soak it in with water for about 3o minutes to an hour before you clean it. If the smell remains, then rub one lemon half over the drawer and the basket. Allow it to soak for another 30 minutes before washing it again.

Please do be careful with any non-stick appliances. They are a wonder for cleaning, but they can flake or come off over time. Be gentle, as you do not want anything to scratch or to even chip the coating. Not only does it ruin a little bit of the aesthetic look, a small part of your air fryer will constantly be struggling with sticky food.

There you have it! The first stepping stones and foundational knowledge of an air fryer. The device you will choose, and how you will use it is up to you, but there are still so many exciting varieties, choices, and options to come!

Bacon, Egg, and Cheese Roll Ups

Prep T: 15 min | Cook T: 15 min | Servings: 4

Ingredients

- 2 tbsp butter
- 32 grams of onion
- 1/2 medium green pepper, seeded and sliced
- 6 large eggs
- 12 slices bacon
- 128 grams of Cheddar cheese
- 64 grams of mild salsa, for soaking

Directions

1. In a medium skillet over medium heat, dissolve butter. Attach onion and pepper to the skillet and sauté until fragrant and onions are translucent, about 3 min.
2. Pour eggs in a bowl and set into a pan.
3. On work surface, set three slices of bacon side by side, overlapping about 0.6 cm. Set 32 grams of scrambled eggs in a heap on the side closest to you and whisk cheese over the eggs.
4. Tightly set the bacon around the eggs. Set each roll into the air fryer basket.
5. Set the temperature to 176 degs C. Set the rolls halfway through the cooking time.
6. Serve immediately with salsa for dipping.

Nutrition: Calories: 460; Protein: 28.2 g; Fiber: 0.8 g; Net Carbohydrates: 5.3 g; Fat: 31.7 g; Sodium: 1,100 mg; Carbohydrates: 6.1 g; Sugar: 3.1 g;

Scrambled Eggs

Prep T: 5 min | Cook T: 15 min | Servings: 2

Ingredients

- 4 large eggs
- 2 tbsp unsalted butter, melted
- 64 grams of shredded sharp Cheddar cheese

Directions

1. Crack eggs into a 256 grams round baking dish and whisk. After that, put the dish into the air fryer basket.
2. Set the temperature to 204 degs C and set the timer for 10 min.

3. After 5 min, stir the eggs and add the butter and cheese. Let cook 3 more min and stir again.
4. Allow eggs to finish cooking an additional 2 min or remove if they are to your desired liking.
5. Use a fork to fluff. Serve warm.

Nutrition: Calories: 359 ; Protein: 19.5 g; Fiber: 0.0 g; Net Carbohydrates: 1.1 g; Fat: 27.6 g; Sodium: 325 mg; Carbohydrates: 1.1 g; Sugar: 0.5 g;

Breakfast Calzone

Prep T: 15 min | Cook T: 15 min | Servings: 4

Ingredients

- 192 grams of shredded mozzarella cheese
- 64 grams of finely ground almond flour
- 28 grams of full-fat cream cheese
- 1 large whole egg
- 4 large eggs, scrambled
- 453 grams of cooked breakfast sausage, crumbled
- 8 tbsp shredded mild Cheddar cheese

Directions

1. Get a microwave-safe bowl and add mozzarella cheese, almond flour and cream cheese inside. Microwave for 1 minute. Mix until the mixture is even and forms a ball then add the egg and mix until the dough forms.
2. Set dough between two sheets of parchment and roll out to 0.6 cm thickness. Cut the dough into four rectangles.
3. Get a container and mix the scrambled egg with the sausage. Place the mixture between each piece of dough, placing it on the bottom half of the rectangle.. Sprinkle each with 2 tbsp Cheddar.
4. Fold over the rectangle to cover the egg and meat mixture. Pinch, roll, or use a wet fork to close the edges completely.
5. Divide a piece of parchment to fit your air fryer basket and place the calzones onto the parchment. Place parchment into the air fryer basket.
6. Set the temperature to 194 degs C and set the timer for 15 min.
7. Flip the calzones halfway through the cooking time. When done, calzones should be golden in color. At that point you can serve.

Nutrition: Calories: 560 Protein: 34.5 g; Fiber: 1.5 g; Net Carbohydrates: 4.2 g; Fat: 41.7 g; Sodium: 930 mg; Carbohydrates: 5.7 g; Sugar: 2.1 g;

Buttermilk Biscuits

Prep T : 5 min | Cook T : 18 min | 16 biscuits

Ingredients:

- 192 grams of all-purpose flour
- 1 tbsp baking powder
- 1 tsp kosher salt
- 1 tsp sugar
- ½ tsp baking soda
- 128 grams of buttermilk, chilled
- 8 tbsp unsalted butter, at room temperature

Directions:

1. Stir together the flour, baking powder, salt, sugar and baking powder in a large bowl.
2. Add the butter and stir to mix well. Pour in the buttermilk and stir with a rubber spatula just until incorporated.
3. Place the dough onto a lightly floured surface and roll the dough out to a disk, 12 mm thick. Cut out the biscuits with a 5 cm round cutter and re-roll any scraps until you have 16 biscuits.
4. Arrange the biscuits in the air fryer basket in a single layer.
5. Place the basket on the bake position.
6. Select Bake, set temperature to 163 degs C, and set time to 18 min.
7. When cooked, the biscuits will be golden brown.
8. Remove from the air fryer grill to a plate and serve hot.

Nutrition: Calories 125; Fat 6.7 g; Carbohydrates 10.7 g; Sugar 3.5 g; Protein 5.2 g;

Coconut Pudding

Prep T: 5 minutes | Cook T: 20 minutes | Servings: 4

Ingredients

- 128 grams of cauliflower rice
- 64 grams of coconut, shredded
- 384 ml coconut milk
- 1 tbsp stevia

Directions

1. In a pan that fits the air fryer, combine all the ingredients and whisk well. Introduce the pan in your air fryer and cook at 182 degs C for 20 minutes.
2. Divide into bowls and serve for breakfast.

Nutrition: Calories: 211; Fat: 11g; Fiber: 3g; Carbs: 4g; Protein:8g

Cheese Sandwich

Prep T: 15 minutes | Cook T: 3 minutes | Servings: 2

Ingredients

- 2 low carb tortillas
- 2 Cheddar cheese slices
- 2 deli ham slices
- 2 lettuce leaves
- 2 tsps mascarpone
- ¼ tsp chives, chopped

Directions

1. Cut every tortilla into halves. In the shallow bowl mix up chives and mascarpone. Spread the tortilla halves with mascarpone mixture. Then place cheese and ham on 2 tortilla halves. Add leaves and top them with remaining tortilla halves.
2. Preheat the air fryer to 205 degs C. Place the tortilla sandwiches in the air fryer and cook them for 3 minutes at 205 degs C.

Nutrition: Calories: 248; Fat: 14.4g; Fiber: 8.4g; Carbs: 13.8g; Protein:15.2g

Strawberries and Coconut Mix

Prep T: 5 minutes cooking time: 15 minutes 4

Ingredients

- 128 ml coconut milk
- 32 grams of strawberries
- ¼ tsp vanilla extract
- 64 grams of coconut, shredded
- 2 tsps stevia Cooking Spray

Directions

1. Grease the Air Fryer's pan with the cooking spray, add all the ingredients inside and toss. Cook at 185 degs C for 15 minutes, divide into bowls and serve for breakfast.

Nutrition: Calories: 142; Fat: 7g; Fiber: 2g; Carbs: 3g; Protein:5g

Bacon Pockets

Prep T: 15 minutes | Cook T: 4 minutes | Servings: 6

Ingredients

- 6 wontons wrap
- 1 egg yolk, whisked
- 57 grams bacon, chopped, cooked
- 64 grams of Edam cheese, shredded
- 1 tsp sesame oil
- ½ tsp ground black pepper

Directions

1. Put the chopped bacon in the bowl. Add Edam cheese and ground black pepper. Stir the ingredients gently with the help of the fork. After this, put the mixture on the wonton wrap and fold it in the shape of the pocket.
2. Repeat the steps with remaining filling and wonton wraps. Preheat the air fryer to 205 degs C. Brush every wonton pocket with whisked egg yolk. Then brush the air fryer with

sesame oil and arrange the pockets inside. Cook the meal for 2 minutes from each side.

Nutrition: Calories: 136; Fat: 10.1g; Fiber: 0.1g; Carbs: 2.6g; Protein:8.6g

Portobello Eggs Benedict

Prep T: 10 min | Cook T: 14 min | Servings: 2

Ingredients

- 1 tbsp olive oil
- 1 cloves garlic, minced
- 1/4 tsp dried thyme
- 2 Portobello mushrooms, stems removed and gills scraped out
- 2 Roma tomatoes, halved lengthwise
- Salt and ground black pepper, to taste
- 2 large eggs
- 2 tbsp grated Pecorino Romano cheese
- 1 tbsp chopped fresh parsley, for garnish
- 1 tsp truffle oil (optional)

Directions

1. Preheat the air fryer to 204 degs C.
2. In a small bowl, merge the olive oil, garlic, and thyme. Brush the mixture over the mushrooms and tomatoes until thoroughly coated. Flavour to taste with salt and freshly ground black pepper.
3. Arrange the vegetables, cut side up, in the air fryer basket. Set an egg into the center of each mushroom and sprinkle with cheese. Air fry for 10 to 14 min until the vegetables are tender and the whites are firm. When cool enough to handle, slice the tomatoes and set on top of the eggs. Scatter parsley on top and drizzle with truffle oil, if desired, just before serving.

Nutrition: Calories: 255; Fat: 20g; Protein: 11g; Carbs: 10g; Net Carbs: 7g; Fiber: 3g;

Turkey Sausage Breakfast Pizza

Prep T: 10 min | Cook T: 24 min | Servings: 2

Ingredients

- 4 large eggs, divided
- 1 tbsp water
- 1/2 tsp garlic powder
- 1/2 tsp onion powder
- 1/2 tsp dried oregano
- 2 tbsp coconut flour
- 3 tbsp grated Parmesan cheese
- 64 grams of shredded provolone cheese
- 1 link cooked turkey sausage, chopped (57 g)
- 2 sun-dried tomatoes, finely chopped
- 2 scallions, thinly sliced

Directions

1. Preheat the air fryer to 204 degs C. Set a cake pan with parchment paper and lightly coat the paper with olive oil.
2. In a large bowl, whisk 2 of the eggs with the water, garlic powder, onion powder, and dried oregano. Add the coconut flour, breaking up any lumps with your hands as you add it to the bowl. Toss the coconut flour into the egg mixture, mixing until smooth. Stir in the Parmesan cheese. Set the mixture to rest for a few min until thick and dough-like.

3. Transfer the mixture to the prepared pan. Use a spatula to scatter it evenly and slightly up the sides of the pan. Air fry until the crust is set but still light in color, about 10 min. Top with the cheeses, sausage, and sun-dried tomatoes.
4. Break the remaining eggs into a bowl, and then slide them onto the pizza. Return the pizza to the air fryer. Air fry 10 to 14 min until the egg whites are set and the yolks are the desired doneness. Top with the scallions and allow to rest for 5 min before serving.

Nutrition: Calories: 345; Fat: 23g; Protein: 29g; Carbs: 5g; Net Carbs: 4g; Fiber: 1g;

Ham Breakfast

Prep T: 10 min | Cook T: 15 min | Servings: 6

Ingredients

- 768 grams of French bread, cubed
- 113 grams of green chilies, chopped
- 283 grams ham, cubed
- 114 grams cheddar cheese, shredded
- 256 ml milk
- 5 eggs
- 1 tbsp mustard
- Salt and black pepper to the taste
- Cooking Spray

Directions

1. Warm up your air fryer at 176 degs C and grease it with cooking spray.
2. In a bowl, mix eggs with milk, cheese, mustard, salt and pepper and stir.
3. Attach bread cubes in your air fryer and mix with chilies and ham.
4. Add eggs mix, spread and cook for 15 min.
5. Divide among plates and serve.
6. Enjoy!

Nutrition: Calories 200; Fat 5g; Fiber 6g; Carbs 12g; Protein 14g;

Easy Sausage Quiche

Prep T: 5 min | Cook T: 25 min | Servings: 4

Ingredients

- 12 large eggs
- 128 grams of heavy cream
- Salt and black pepper, to taste
- 258 grams of shredded Cheddar cheese
- 340 grams sugar-free breakfast sausage

- Cooking Spray

Directions

1. Coat a casserole dish with cooking spray.
2. Beat together the eggs, heavy cream, salt and pepper in a large bowl until creamy. Stir in the breakfast sausage and Cheddar cheese.
3. Pour the sausage mixture into the prepared casserole dish.
4. Place the dish on the bake position. Select Bake, set temperature to 190 degs C and set time to 25 min.
5. When done, the top of the quiche should be golden brown and the eggs will be set.
6. Remove from the air fryer grill and let sit for 5 to 10 min before serving.

Nutrition: Calories 740; Fat 59 g; Carbohydrates 3.5 g; Sugar 1.2 g; Protein 44.25 g;

Sausage Egg Cup

Prep T: 10 min | Cook T: 15 min | Servings: 6

Ingredients

- 340 g ground pork breakfast sausage
- 6 eggs
- 1/2 tsp salt
- 1/4 tsp ground black pepper
- 1/2 tsp crushed red pepper flakes

Directions

1. Place sausage in six 10 cm ramekins (about 57 g per ramekin) greased with cooking oil. Press sausage down to cover bottom and about 1.3 cm up the sides of ramekins. Beat one egg into each ramekin and sprinkle evenly with salt, black pepper, and red pepper flakes.
2. Place ramekins into air fryer basket. Set the temperature to 180 degs C and set the timer for 15 min. Egg cups will be done when sausage is fully cooked to at least 63 degs C and the egg is firm. Serve warm.

Nutrition: Calories: 267 ; Fat: 21g; Protein:14g; Carbs: 1g; Net Carbs: 1g; Fiber: 0g

Tender Muffins

Prep T: 15 min | Cook T: 12 min | Servings: 4

Ingredients

- 4 slices of ham, chopped
- 4 eggs, beaten
- 32 grams of coconut cream
- 1 tsp dried dill
- 1 tsp coconut oil, softened
- 1/2 tsp chives, chopped

Directions

1. In the mixing bowl, mix ham with eggs, coconut cream, dried dill, coconut oil, and chives.
2. Put the mixture in the muffin molds and bake at 185 degs C for 12 min.

Nutrition: Calories: 153; Fat: 11.5g; Fiber: 0.7g; Carbs: 2.4g; Protein:10.6g

Breakfast Casserole

Prep T: 21 min | Cook T: 35 min | Servings: 4

Ingredients

- 2 eggs

- 4 egg whites
- 4 tsp. pine nuts, minced
- 85 ml chicken broth
- 453 grams of Italian sausage
- 32 grams of roasted red pepper, sliced
- 32 grams of pesto sauce
- 85 grams of parmesan cheese, grated
- 1/8 tsp. pepper
- 1/4 tsp. sea salt

Directions

1. Preheat the air fryer to 187 degs C.
2. Spray air fryer pan and set aside.
3. Heat another pan over medium heat. Add sausage to a pan and cook until golden brown.
4. Once cooked then drain excess oil and spread it into the prepared pan.
5. Whisk remaining ingredients except pine nuts in a bowl and pour over sausage.
6. Cook for 25-28 min.
7. Top with pine nuts and serve.

Nutrition: Calories 623; Fat 49.4 g; Carbohydrates 2 g; Sugar 9.4 g; Protein 39 g; Cholesterol 0 mg;

Cheddar and Ham Quiche

Prep T: 10 minutes | Cook T: 15 minutes | Servings: 4

Ingredients

- 114 grams ham, chopped
- 128 grams of Cheddar cheese, shredded
- 1 tbsp chives, chopped
- ½ zucchini, grated
- 32 grams of heavy cream
- 1 tbsp almond flour
- ½ tsp salt
- ½ tsp ground black pepper
- ½ tsp dried oregano
- 5 eggs, beaten
- 1 tsp coconut oil, softened

Directions

1. In the big bowl mix up ham, cheese, chives, zucchini, heavy cream, almond flour, salt, ground black pepper, oregano, and eggs. Stir the ingredients with the help of the fork until you get a homogenous mixture. After this, preheat the air fryer to 185 degs C. Then gently grease the air fryer basket with coconut oil.
2. Pour the ham mixture in the air fryer basket.
3. Cook the quiche for 15 minutes. Then check if the quiche mixture is crusty, cook for extra 5 minutes if needed.

Nutrition: Calories: 320 ; Fat: 24.8g ; Fiber: 1.6g ; Carbs: 4.7g ; Protein:20.7g

Cheesy Pancake

Prep T: 10 minutes | Cook T: 8 minutes | Servings: 2

Ingredients

- 5 eggs, beaten
- 32 grams almond flour
- ½ tsp baking powder
- 1 tsp apple cider vinegar
- 32 grams Cheddar cheese, shredded
- 1 tsp butter
- 1 tbsp mascarpone

- ½ tsp sesame oil

Directions

1. Brush the air fryer basket with sesame oil. Then in the mixing bowl mix up all remaining ingredients. Stir the liquid until homogenous. Pour it in the air fryer pan and place it in the air fryer. Cook the pancake for 8 minutes at 182 degs C.
2. Remove the cooked pancake from the air fryer pan and cut it into servings.

Nutrition: Calories: 276; Fat: 21.4g; Fiber: 0.4g; Carbs: 2.6g; Protein:19g

Lemon and Almond Cookies

Prep T: 10 minutes | Cook T: 8 minutes | Servings: 4

Ingredients

- 4 tbsp coconut flour
- ½ tsp baking powder
- 1 tsp lemon juice
- ¼ tsp vanilla extract
- ¼ tsp lemon zest, grated
- 2 eggs, beaten
- 32 ml of organic almond milk
- 1 tsp avocado oil
- ¼ tsp Himalayan pink salt

Directions

1. In the big bowl mix up all ingredients from the list above. Knead the soft dough and cut it into 4 pieces. Preheat the air fryer to 205 degs C. Then line the air fryer basket with baking paper.
2. Roll the dough pieces in the balls and press them gently to get the shape of flat cookies. Place the cookies in the air fryer and cook them for 8 minutes.

Nutrition: Calories: 74; Fat: 3.8g; Fiber: 3.1g; Carbs: 5.6g; Protein:4.4g

Cheesy Sausage Sticks

Prep T: 15 minutes | Cook T: 8 minutes | Servings: 3

Ingredients

- 6 small pork sausages
- 64 grams almond flour
- 64 grams Mozzarella cheese, shredded
- 2 eggs, beaten
- 1 tbsp mascarpone
- Cooking Spray

Directions

1. Pierce the hot dogs with wooden coffee sticks to get the sausages on the sticks. Then in the bowl mix up almond flour, Mozzarella cheese, and mascarpone. Microwave the mixture for 15 seconds or until you get a melted mixture. Then stir the egg in the cheese mixture and whisk it until smooth.
2. Coat every sausage stick in the cheese mixture. Then preheat the air fryer to 190 degs C. Grease the basket of the air fryer with cooking spray.
3. Place the sausage stock in the air fryer and cook them for 4 minutes from each side or until they are light brown.

Nutrition: Calories: 375; Fat: 32.2g; Fiber: 0.5g; Carbs: 5.1g; Protein:16.3g

Grilled Cheese Sandwich

Prep T: 5 minutes | Cook T: 5 minutes | Servings: 1

Ingredients

- 2 slices of bread
- 2 slices of turkey
- 2 slices of cheddar
- 15 grams of butter

Directions

1. Preheat the air fryer to 180 degs C.
2. Spread the butter on the slices of bread.
3. Place the turkey and cheese slices on a slice of bread.
4. Cover the sandwich with the other slice of bread.
5. Place the sandwich in the basket of the air fryer and cook for 5 minutes.
6. Serve and enjoy your meal

Nutrition: Calories: 546; Fat: 28 g; Fiber: 1 g; Carbs: 36 g; Protein: 32 g

Banana Muffin

Prep T: 10 minutes | Cook T: 10 minutes | Servings: 12

Ingredients

- 1 egg
- 250 grams of all-purpose flour
- 80 grams of butter, melted
- 1 teaspoon of cinnamon
- 150 grams of sugar
- 3 bananas, mashed
- 1 teaspoon of baking soda
- 1 teaspoon of baking powder
- 1/2 teaspoon of salt

Directions

1. Preheat the air fryer to 180 degs C.
2. Put all the ingredients in a blender and blend them until well blended.
3. Pour the batter into the silicone muffin molds.
4. Place the muffin tins in the air fryer basket and cook for 10 minutes.
5. Serve and enjoy your meal!

Nutrition: Calories: 189; Fat: 6 g; Fiber: 2 g; Carbs: 20 g; Protein: 10 g; Sugar: 12g

Omelette with Broccoli and Mushrooms

Prep T: 10 minutes | Cook T: 10 minutes | Servings: 2

Ingredients

- 2 eggs
- 2 tablespoons of milk
- 70 grams Mexican cheese, chopped
- 50 grams of mushrooms, sliced
- 50 grams broccoli tops, stewed
- pepper
- salt

Directions

1. In a bowl, beat eggs with milk, pepper and salt.
2. Incorporate cheese, mushrooms and broccoli and mix well.
3. Pour the egg mixture into the greased pan of the air fryer.
4. Place the pan in the basket of the air fryer and cook at 160 degs C for 8-10 minutes.
5. Slice and serve.

Nutrition: Calories: 266; Fat: 17 g; Fiber: 1 g; Carbs: 7 g; Protein: 16.5 g; Sugar: 3.5 g

Greek omelette

Prep T: 10 minutes | Cook T: 25 minutes | Servings: 1

Ingredients

- 4 eggs
- 230 g baby spinach, chopped
- 1/2 teaspoon of chili peppers
- 1 teaspoon of black pepper
- 80 ml of Greek yogurt
- 2 tablespoons of parsley, chopped
- 2 tablespoons of celery, chopped
- 2 tablespoons of carrot, chopped
- 2 tablespoons of onion, chopped
- 1/2 teaspoon of olive oil

Directions

1. Preheat the air fryer to 180 degs C.
2. Add oil, onion, parsley, celery and carrot to the pan of the air fryer and mix well.
3. Place the pan in the basket of the air fryer and cook for 5 minutes.
4. Meanwhile, mix the eggs, yogurt, pepper, red chillies, and spinach in a bowl until everything is combined well.
5. Pour the egg mixture into the pan and place it in the air fryer basket and cook for 18-20 minutes.
6. Slice and serve

Nutrition: Calories: 379; Fat: 19 g; Protein: 38 g; Carbs: 10 g; Fiber: 4 g; Sugar: 2 g

Garlic bread with cheese

Prep T: 10 minutes | Cook T: 5 minutes | Servings: 4

Ingredients

- 1 baguette, cut into 2 cm thick slices
- 240 grams of Parmesan, grated
- 10 cloves of garlic, minced
- 1 teaspoon of peppercorns, crushed
- 1 teaspoon of oregano
- 60 grams of butter, melted
- 60 ml of milk
- 20 g of fresh parsley, chopped

Directions

1. In a small bowl, mix the butter, chili peppers, oregano, parsley, milk, and garlic.
2. Brush one side of each baguette slice with the butter mixture and sprinkle it with grated cheese.
3. Place the baguette slices in the basket of the air fryer and cook at 180 degs C for 5 minutes.
4. Serve and enjoy your meal!

Nutrition: Calories: 538; Fat: 30 g; Protein: 24 g; Carbs: 41 g; Fiber: 1 g; Sugar: 3.5 g

Apple French Toast

Prep T: 10 minutes | Cook T: 10 minutes | Servings: 8

Ingredients

- 1 egg, lightly beaten
- 8 slices of bread
- 2 tablespoons of maple syrup
- 6 tablespoons of applesauce
- 11/2 tablespoons of cinnamon
- 1 tablespoon of milk

Directions

1. In a bowl, mix the egg with the milk, cinnamon, applesauce, and maple syrup.
2. Dip each slice of bread in the egg mixture and place them in the basket of the air fryer and cook at 180 degs C for 10 minutes. Bake the slices of bread in batches.
3. Serve and enjoy your meal!

Nutrition: Calories: 414; Fat: 4.5 g; Protein: 17 g; Carbs: 75 g; Fiber: 3.25 g; Sugar: 9.5 g

Fried donuts

Prep T: 10 minutes | Cook T: 9 minutes | Servings: 8

Ingredients

- 2 eggs
- 250 g of pancake mix
- 11/2 tablespoons of cinnamon
- 50 grams of sugar
- 120 ml of vegetable oil

Directions

1. In a bowl, mix the pancake mix with the egg, cinnamon, sugar, and oil until combined.
2. Pour the mixture into silicone donut cups.
3. Place the baking cups in the basket of the air fryer and cook at 180 degs C for 9 minutes.
4. Serve and enjoy your meal!

Nutrition: Calories: 285; Fat: 17 g; Protein: 4.5 g; Carbs: 30 g; Fiber: 0.8 g; Sugar: 11 g

Strawberry Donuts

Prep T: 10 minutes | Cook T: 15 minutes | Servings: 8

Ingredients

- 1 egg
- 85 grams strawberries, diced
- 2 teaspoons of vanilla
- 2 tablespoons of butter, melted
- 70 grams of sugar
- 80 ml of milk
- 1 teaspoon of cinnamon
- 1 teaspoon of baking soda
- 150 grams of multi-purpose flour
- 1/2 teaspoon of salt

Directions

1. In a bowl, combine the flour, baking soda, sugar, cinnamon, and salt.
2. In a separate bowl, whisk the egg, milk, butter, and vanilla.
3. Pour the egg mixture into the flour mixture and mix everything well.
4. Add the strawberries and mix again.
5. Pour the mixture into silicone donut cups.
6. Place the muffin tins in the basket of the air fryer and cook at 160 degs C for 10-15 minutes.
7. Serve and enjoy your meal!

Nutrition: Calories: 138; Fat: 4 g; Protein: 10 g; Carbs: 16 g; Fiber: 0.2 g; Sugar: 9 g

Chocolate Pudding

Prep T: 15 Minutes | Cook T: 10 Minutes | Servings: 2
Ingredients

- 60 ml of butter
- 60 ml of whole milk
- 120 grams of chocolate chips, melted
- 1 egg
- 4 tablespoons of sugar
- Spray oil, for greasing
- 240g of flour

Directions

1. Take a bowl and put the butter in it.
2. Melt it by putting it in the microwave.
3. Mix well and add the sugar and milk.
4. At the end, add egg and flour.
5. Incorporate the melted chocolate chips.
6. Pour this mixture into greased molds.
7. Place the molds in the basket of the air fryer and cook for 10 minutes at 40 degs C.
8. When ready, serve and enjoy.
9. The internal consistency will be liquid.

Nutrition: Calories: 800; Fat: 46 g; Protein: 31 g; Carbs: 64 g; Fiber: 4 g; Sugar: 36 g

Sandwich with Provolone and Ham

Prep T: 8 Minutes | Cook T: 10 Minutes | Serving: 1
Ingredients

- 2 slices of bread
- 1 tablespoon of butter
- 2 slices of provolone
- 2 slices of ham

Directions

1. Preheat the air fryer to 200 degs C for a few minutes.
2. Spread the butter on the slices of bread.
3. Place the bread in the basket of the air fryer and cover it with cheese and ham.
4. Cover with the other slice.
5. Cook for 6-10 minutes, turn the sandwich halfway through cooking.
6. When ready, serve and enjoy.

Nutrition: Calories: 900; Fat: 20 g; Protein: 35 g; Carbs: 144 g; Fiber: 6 g; Sugar: 12 g

Avocado Toast

Prep T: 12 Minutes | Cook T: 10 Minutes | Servings: 2
Ingredients

- 1 large avocado, pitted
- 1 tablespoon of lemon juice
- Salt to taste.
- A pinch of paprika
- 2 slices of cereal bread
- 1 tablespoon of butter
- 2 eggs
- Spray oil, for greasing

Directions

1. The first step is to pit the avocados and put them in a bowl, then add the lemon juice, paprika and salt.
2. Spread the butter on the bread and spread the avocado puree on the other slice.
3. Place the bread, butter side down, into the basket of the air fryer.
4. Cook for 10 minutes at 175 degs C.
5. Meanwhile, break the eggs into a pan and cook them in butter if desired, then serve over the toast.
6. Enjoy your meal.

Nutrition: Calories: 270; Fat: 20 g; Protein: 8.5 g; Carbs: 11 g; Fiber: 5 g; Sugar: 0 g

Hard-boiled eggs

Prep T: 15 Minutes | Cook T: 10-15 Minutes | Servings: 2
Ingredients

- 1-6 large eggs

Directions

1. Preheat the air fryer to 100 degs C for a few minutes.
2. Place the eggs in the air fryer and cook for 15 minutes at 140 degs C.
3. When cooked, remove the eggs and soak them in cold water.
4. Peel the eggs and let them cool enough to slice and serve.
5. Cook for 10 minutes to make hard-boiled eggs.

Nutrition: Calories: 71; Fat: 4 g; Protein:6 g; Carbs: 0 g; Fiber: 0 g; Sugar: 0 g

Yogurt pancakes

Prep T: 15 Minutes | Cook T: 8-16 Minutes | Servings: 2
Ingredients

- 180 grams of flour 00
- 120 ml of Greek yogurt
- 1 egg
- 60 grams of sugar
- ½ teaspoon of baking soda
- ¼ teaspoon of salt
- 120 grams of cottage cheese
- ½ teaspoon of vanilla extract
- ½ teaspoon of lemon extract

- Fruit to taste

Directions

1. Combine flour, baking soda, sugar and salt in a bowl.
2. Take another bowl and beat the eggs into it.
3. Add the Greek yogurt, lemon, cottage cheese, vanilla to the egg, then add the flour mixture to the yogurt.
4. Take a cake pan and line it with baking paper.
5. Take a small glass and fill it with dough.
6. Pour the dough into the pan a little at a time
7. Place the cake pan in the air fryer.
8. Cook for 6 minutes at 150 degs C.
9. Repeat until all the dough is used up.
10. When the pancakes are ready, serve and enjoy with the fruit topping.

Nutrition: Calories: 549; Fat: 6.5 g; Protein:27 g; Carbs: 97 g; Fiber: 9.5 g; Sugar: 32 g

Cheesy Green Chiles Nachos

Prep T: 10 min | Cook T: 10 min | Servings: 6

Ingredients

- 227 g tortilla chips
- 384 grams of shredded Monterey Jack cheese, divided
- 396 grams of cans chopped green chiles, drained
- 227 grams can tomato sauce
- ¼ tsp dried oregano
- ¼ tsp granulated garlic
- ¼ tsp freshly ground black pepper
- Pinch cinnamon
- Pinch cayenne pepper

Directions

1. Arrange the tortilla chips close together in a single layer on the sheet pan.
2. Sprinkle 128 – 64 grams of the cheese over the chips. Arrange the green chiles over the cheese as evenly as possible. Top with the remaining 192 grams of the cheese.
3. Place the pan on the toast position.
4. Select Toast, set temperature to 190 degs C and set time to 10 min.
5. After 5 min, rotate the pan and continue cooking.
6. Meanwhile, stir together the remaining ingredients in a bowl.
7. When cooking is complete, the cheese will be melted and starting to crisp around the edges of the pan. Remove the pan from the air fryer grill. Drizzle the sauce over the nachos and serve warm.

Nutrition: Calories 402; Fat 26 g; Carbohydrates 24 g; Protein 17 g; Fiber 1.8 g;

Garlic Asparagus

Prep T: 10 minutes | Cook T: 5 minutes | Servings: 3

Ingredients

- 255 grams of Asparagus
- ¼ tsp chili powder
- ¼ tsp garlic powder
- 1 tsp olive oil
- 4 Provolone cheese slices

Directions

1. Trim the asparagus and sprinkle with chili powder and garlic powder. Then preheat the air fryer to 205 degs C. Put the asparagus in the air fryer basket and sprinkle with olive oil.
2. Cook the vegetables for 3 minutes. Then top the asparagus with Provolone cheese and cook for 3 minutes more.

Nutrition: Calories: 163; Fat: 11.6g; Fiber: 1.9g; Carbs: 4.4g; Protein:11.5g

Cheese Broccoli

Prep T: 10 minutes | Cook T: 7 minutes | Servings: 4

Ingredients

- 128 grams broccoli, chopped, boiled
- 1 tsp nut oil
- 1 tsp salt
- 1 tsp dried basil
- 64 grams Cheddar cheese, shredded
- 64 ml of coconut milk
- ½ tsp butter, softened

Directions

1. Put broccoli in the air fryer pan. Add nut oil, salt, and dried dill. Stir the vegetables well and add coconut milk. Then add butter and top the meal with Cheddar cheese. Stir the meal gently.
2. Preheat the air fryer to 205 degs C and put the pan with the vegetable mixture inside. Cook it for 7 minutes.

Nutrition: Calories: 154; Fat: 13.6g; Fiber: 1.9g; Carbs: 4.7g; Protein:5.4g

Crispy Spiced Potatoes

Prep T: 10 min | Cook T: 20 min | Servings: 4

Ingredients:

- 907 grams of baby red potatoes, quartered
- 2 tbsp extra-virgin olive oil
- 32 grams dried onion flakes
- 1 tsp dried rosemary
- ½ tsp onion powder
- ½ tsp garlic powder
- ¼ tsp celery powder
- ¼ tsp freshly ground black pepper

- ½ tsp dried parsley
- ½ tsp sea salt

Directions:

1. Place the crisper tray on the air fry position. Select Air Fry, set the temperature to 199 degs C, and set the time to 20 min.
2. Meanwhile, place all the ingredients in a large bowl and toss until evenly coated.
3. Add the potatoes to the crisper tray. Air fry for 10 min.
4. After 10 min, shake the crisper tray well. Place the crisper tray back in the grill to resume cooking.
5. After 10 min, check for desired crispness. Continue cooking up to 5 min more, if necessary.

Nutrition: Calories 217; Fat 7 g; Carbohydrates 36 g; Protein 4 g; Fiber 4 g; Sugar 3 g;

Italian Eggplant Bites

Prep T: 10 minutes | Cook T: 10 minutes | Servings: 5

Ingredients

- 2 medium eggplants, trimmed
- 1 tomato
- 1 tsp Italian seasonings
- 1 tsp avocado oil
- 85 grams of Parmesan, sliced

Directions

1. Slice the eggplants on 5 slices. Then thinly slice the tomato on 5 slices. Place the eggplants in the air fryer in one layer and cook for 3 minutes from every side at 205 degs C. After this, top the sliced eggplants with tomato, sprinkle with avocado oil and Italian seasonings. Then top the eggplants with Parmesan.
2. Cook the meal for 4 minutes at 205 degs C.

Nutrition: Calories: 116; Fat: 4.5g; Fiber: 7.9g; Carbs: 14.1g; Protein:7.7g

Bruschetta with Tomato and Basil

Prep T: 5 min | Cook T: 6 min | Servings: 6

Ingredients:

- 4 tomatoes, diced
- 43 grams of shredded fresh basil
- 32 grams shredded Parmesan cheese
- 1 tbsp balsamic vinegar
- 1 tbsp minced garlic
- 1 tsp olive oil

- 1 tsp salt
- 1 tsp freshly ground black pepper
- 1 loaf French bread, cut into 2-cm-thick slices
- Cooking Spray

Directions:

1. Place the crisper tray on the bake position. Select Bake, set the temperature to 121 degs C, and set the time to 3 min.
2. Get a bowl and mix in the tomatoes, basil, cheese, vinegar, garlic, olive oil, salt and pepper until well incorporated. Set aside.
3. Spritz the crisper tray with cooking spray. Working in batches, lay the bread slices in the crisper tray in a single layer. Spray the slices with cooking spray.
4. Bake for 3 min until golden brown.
5. Remove from the crisper tray to a plate. Repeat with the remaining bread slices.
6. Top each slice with a generous spoonful of the tomato mixture and serve.

Nutrition: Calories 48; Fat 2.3 g; Carbohydrates 6,6 g; Protein 1,3 g; Fiber 0 g; Sugar 4,83 g;

Jalapeño Poppers

Prep T: 10 min | Cook T: 15 min | Servings: 8

Ingredients:

- 12 large jalapeño peppers (about 5 cm long)
- 170 grams of cream cheese, at room temperature
- 1 tsp chili powder
- 113 grams of shredded Cheddar cheese
- 2 slices cooked bacon, chopped fine
- 32 grams panko bread crumbs
- 1 tbsp butter, melted

Directions:

1. If the jalapeños have stems, cut them off flush with the tops of the chiles. Slice the jalapeños in two lengthwise and scoop the seeds out. For milder poppers, remove the white membranes (the ribs). (You should probably wear latex gloves when you do this, to avoid possible burns. I often forget, and I often regret it.)
2. In a bowl, mix the cream cheese, chili powder, and Cheddar cheese. Spoon the cheese mixture into the jalapeño halves and place them in the baking pan. If the jalapeños roll or tip,

use a vegetable peeler to scrape away a thin layer of skin on the base so they're more stable.

3. In a small bowl, stir together the bacon, panko, and butter. Top each of the jalapeño halves with the panko mixture.
4. Place the pan on the roast position. Select Roast, set temperature to 191 degs C, and set time to 15 min.
5. After 7 or 8 min, rotate the pan 180 degs and continue cooking until the peppers have softened somewhat, the filling is bubbling, and the panko is browned.
6. When cooking is done, remove from grill. Let the poppers cool down for a few min before serving.

Nutrition: Calories 178; Fat 14 g; Carbohydrates 4 g; Protein 9 g; Fiber 0.5 g; Sugar 1 g;

Crispy Avocado Chips

Prep T: 15 min | Cook T: 10 min | Servings: 4

Ingredients:

- 1 egg
- 1 tbsp lime juice
- 1/8 tsp hot sauce
- 2 tbsp flour
- 96 grams of panko bread crumbs
- 32 grams cornmeal
- 1/4 tsp salt
- 1 large avocado, pitted, peeled, and cut into 1.2 cm slices
- Cooking Spray

Directions:

1. Whisk together the egg, hot sauce, and lime juice in a small bowl.
2. Place now the flour on a sheet of wax paper. In a separate sheet of wax paper, combine the cornmeal, bread crumbs, and salt.
3. Dredge the avocado slices one at a time in the flour, then in the egg mixture, finally roll them in the bread crumb mixture to coat well.
4. Place the breaded avocado slices in the air fry basket and mist them with cooking spray.
5. Place the basket on the air fry position.
6. Select Air Fry, set to 199 degs C, and set time to 10 min.
7. When cooking is complete, the slices should be nicely browned and crispy. Transfer the avocado slices to a plate and serve.

Nutrition: Calories 232; Fat 10 g; Carbohydrates 27.5 g; Protein 7 g; Fiber 5.5 g; Sugar 3 g;

Eggplant Parmesan

Prep T: 10 min | Cook T: 40 min | Servings: 4
Ingredients

- 1 large eggplant,
- 64 grams whole wheat bread crumbs
- 3 tbsp finely grated parmesan cheese
- Salt, to taste
- 1 tsp Italian seasoning mix
- 3 tbsp whole wheat flour
- 1 free-range egg
- 1 tbsp water
- Olive oil spray
- 128 grams marinara sauce
- 32 grams grated mozzarella cheese
- Fresh parsley or basil to garnish

Directions

1. Set your air fryer to 182 degs C.
2. Merge the flour, egg and water in a large bowl.
3. Add the breadcrumbs, parmesan, Italian seasoning and salt in a shallow bowl. Mix properly to combine.
4. Put the eggplant into the egg mixture, drip off any excess, place into the breadcrumbs and coat evenly.
5. Cook in the air fryer until perfectly cooked.

Nutrition: Calories: 193; Net carbs: 24g; Protein: 6g; Fat: 4g

Cheese Sticks

Prep T: 15 min | Cook T: 17 min | Servings: 8
Ingredients

- 8 regular cheese sticks
- 1 large free-range egg
- 32 grams almond flour
- 64 grams grated parmesan cheese
- 1 tsp Italian seasoning
- 1/4 tsp ground rosemary
- 1 tsp garlic powder

Directions

1. Whisk the egg properly in a bowl.
2. Add the almond flour, parmesan, Italian seasoning, and rosemary and garlic powder in another bowl. Mix well to combine properly.
3. Coat the cheese sticks with the egg by dipping it in the egg, drip off any excess and dip in the almond flour.
4. Line a baking pan with a baking sheet. Place the cheese sticks in the pan and place in the freezer for 10 min.
5. Heat the air fryer to 188 degs C.
6. Set out the cheese sticks from the freezer then place in the air fryer.
7. Cook for 10 min, then serve and enjoy.

Nutrition: Calories: 62; Net carbs: 2g; Protein: 4g; Fat: 4g;

Crispy Zucchini Rounds

Prep T: 5 min | Cook T: 14 min | Servings: 4

Ingredients

- 2 zucchini, sliced into 6.35- to 12.7-mm-thick rounds (about 256 grams)
- ¼ tsp garlic granules
- ⅛ tsp sea salt
- Freshly ground black pepper, to taste (optional)
- Cooking Spray

Directions

1. Spritz the air fry basket with cooking spray.
2. Put the zucchini rounds in the air fry basket, spreading them out as much as possible. Top with a sprinkle of sea salt, garlic granules, and black pepper (if desired). Spritz the zucchini rounds with cooking spray.
3. Place the basket on the toast position.
4. Select Toast, set temperature to 200 degs C, and set time to 14 min. Flip the zucchini rounds halfway through.
5. When cooking is complete, the zucchini rounds should be crisp-tender. Remove from the air fryer grill. Let them rest for 5 min and serve.

Nutrition: Calories 75; Fat 3 g; Carbohydrates 12 g; Protein 5 g; Fiber 3 g; Sugar 12 g;

Turmeric Tofu

Prep T: 10 minutes | Cook T: 9 minutes | Servings: 2

Ingredients

- 170 grams of tofu, cubed
- 1 tsp avocado oil
- 1 tsp apple cider vinegar
- 1 garlic clove, diced
- ¼ tsp ground turmeric
- ¼ tsp ground paprika
- ½ tsp dried cilantro
- ¼ tsp lemon zest, grated

Directions

1. In the bowl mix up avocado oil, apple cider vinegar, diced garlic, ground turmeric, paprika, cilantro, and lime zest. Coat the tofu cubes in the oil mixture. Preheat the air fryer to 205 degs C.
2. Put the tofu cubes in the air fryer and cook them for 9 minutes. Shake the tofu cubes from time to time during cooking.

Nutrition: Calories: 67; Fat: 3.9g; Fiber: 1.1g; Carbs: 2.5g; Protein:7.2g

French Fries

Prep T: 15 min | Cook T: 25 min | Servings: 4

Ingredients:

- 454 grams russet or Idaho potatoes, cut in 5 cm strips
- 3 tbsp canola oil

Directions:

1. Place the potatoes in a bowl and cover them with cold water. Let soak for 30 min. Drain well, then pat with a paper towel until very dry.
2. Place the crisper tray on the air fry position. Select Air Fry, set temp to 199 degs C, and set the time to 25 min.
3. Meanwhile, in a large bowl, toss the potatoes with the oil.
4. Add the potatoes to the crisper tray. Air fry for 10 min.
5. After 10 min, shake the crisper tray well. Place the crisper tray back in the grill to resume cooking.
6. After 10 min, check for desired crispness. Continue cooking up to 5 min more, if necessary. When cooking is complete, you can serve with your favorite dipping sauce.

Nutrition: Calories 169; Fat 10.5 g; Carbohydrates 17 g; Protein 2 g; Fiber 2 g; Sugar 0.3 g;

Broccoli Puree

Prep T: 5 minutes | Cook T: 20 minutes | Servings: 4

Ingredients

- 566 grams of broccoli florets
- A drizzle of olive oil
- 4 tbsp basil, chopped
- 85 grams of butter, melted
- 1 garlic clove, minced
- A pinch of salt and black pepper

Directions

1. In a bowl, mix the broccoli with the oil, salt and pepper, toss and transfer to your air fryer's basket.
2. Cook at 194 degs C for 20 minutes, cool the broccoli down and put it in a blender. Add the rest of the ingredients, pulse, divide the mash between plates and serve as a side dish.

Nutrition: Calories: 200; Fat: 14g; Fiber: 3g; Carbs: 6g; Protein:7g

Salmon Bites

Prep T: 5 min | Cook T: 10 min | Servings: 6

Ingredients

- 453 grams of salmon fillet, roughly chopped
- 1 tbsp avocado oil
- 1 tsp dried basil
- 1 tsp ground black pepper

Directions

1. Mix chopped salmon with dried basil and ground black pepper.
2. Put the fish pieces in the air fryer basket and sprinkle with avocado oil.
3. Cook the salmon bites at 190 degs C for 10 min.

Nutrition: Calories 104; Fat 5g; Fiber 0.2g; Carbs 0.4g; Protein 14.7g;

Onion Rings

Prep T: 10 min | Cook T: 10 min | Servings: 3

Ingredients

- 2 white onions, sliced into rings
- 128 grams flour
- 2 eggs, beaten
- 128 grams breadcrumbs

Directions

1. Cover the onion rings with flour.
2. Dip in the egg.
3. Dredge with breadcrumbs.
4. Add to the air fryer.
5. Set it to air fry.
6. Cook at 205 degs C for 10 min.

Serving Suggestions: Serve with tartar sauce.

Prep & Cooking Tips: Make ahead of time and freeze. Air fry when ready to serve.

Nutrition: Calories 415; Fat 7 g; Carbohydrates 66 g; Protein 19 g; Fiber 8 g; Sugar 8.5 g;

Zucchini Fritters

Prep T: 10 minutes | Cook T: 10 minutes | Servings: 4

Ingredients

- 2 zucchinis, grated
- 114 grams of Blue cheese
- 1 egg, beaten
- 1 tbsp flax meal
- 1 tsp dried cilantro
- ¼ tsp salt
- 32 grams spring onions, chopped
- 1 tsp olive oil
- 85 grams of celery stalk, diced
- 1 tbsp coconut flour

Directions

1. Crumble Blue cheese and mix it up with grated zucchini. Add egg, flax meal, dried cilantro, salt, spring onions, diced celery stalk, and coconut flour. Then stir the ingredients with the help of the spoon until homogenous.
2. Make the fritters and sprinkle them with olive oil. After this, preheat the air fryer to 205 degs C.
3. Place the zucchini fritters in the air fryer and cook them for 5 minutes. Then flip the fritters on another side and cook for 5 minutes more or until they are golden brown.

Nutrition: Calories: 164; Fat: 11.6g; Fiber: 2.8g; Carbs: 6.9g; Protein:9.6g

Breaded Green Olives

Prep T: 5 min | Cook T: 8 min | Servings: 4

Ingredients

- 156 grams of jar pitted green olives

- 64 grams all-purpose flour
- Salt and pepper, to taste
- 64 grams bread crumbs
- 1 egg
- Cooking Spray

Directions

1. Place the crisper tray on the air fry position. Select Air Fry, set temp to 204 degs C, and set the time to 8 min.
2. Remove the olives from the jar and dry thoroughly with paper towels.
3. In a small bowl, combine the flour with salt and pepper to taste. Place the bread crumbs in another small bowl. In a third small bowl, beat the egg.
4. Spritz the crisper tray with cooking spray.
5. Dip the olives in the flour, then the egg, and then the bread crumbs.
6. Place the breaded olives in the crisper tray. It is okay to stack them. Spray the olives with cooking spray. Air fry for 6 min. Flip the olives and air fry for an additional 2 min, or until brown and crisp.
7. Cool before serving.

Nutrition: Calories 185; Fat 7.5 g; Carbohydrates 20 g; Protein 7 g; Fiber 3 g; Sugar 0.7 g;

Lemon and Butter Artichok

Prep T: 5 minutes | Cook T: 15 minutes | Servings: 4

Ingredients

- 340 grams of artichoke hearts
- Juice of ½ lemon
- 4 tbsp butter, melted
- 2 tbsp tarragon, chopped
- Salt and black pepper to the taste

Directions

1. In a bowl, mix all the ingredients, toss, transfer the artichokes to your air fryer's basket and cook at 188 degs C for 15 minutes.
2. Prepare the portions and serve them as a side dish.

Nutrition: Calories: 200; Fat: 7g; Fiber: 2g; Carbs: 3g; Protein:7g

Cauliflower Patties

Prep T: 15 minutes | Cook T: 10 minutes | Servings: 2

Ingredients

- 32 grams of cauliflower, shredded
- 1 egg yolk
- ½ tsp ground turmeric
- ¼ tsp onion powder
- ¼ tsp salt
- 56 grams of Cheddar cheese, shredded
- ¼ tsp baking powder
- 1 tsp heavy cream
- Cooking Spray

Directions

1. Squeeze the shredded cauliflower and put it in the bowl. Add egg yolk, ground turmeric, onion powder, baking powder, salt, heavy cream, and coconut flakes. Then melt Cheddar cheese and add it in the cauliflower mixture.

2. Stir the ingredients until you get the smooth mass. After this, make the medium size cauliflower patties. Preheat the air fryer to 185 degs C.
3. Grease the basket of the air fryer with cooking spray and put the patties inside. Cook them for 5 minutes from each side.

Nutrition: Calories: 165; Fat: 13.5g; Fiber: 0.7g; Carbs: 2.7g; Protein:8.9g

Flavoured Air Fried Tomatoes

Prep T: 31 min | Cook T: 15 min | Servings: 4

Ingredients

- garlic cloves, minced
- oregano, dried (1/2 tsp)
- black pepper and salt
- olive oil (32 grams)
- Cherry tomatoes, halved (907 grams)
- basil, chopped (32 grams)
- 1 jalapeno pepper, chopped
- parmesan, grated (64 grams)

Directions

1. Mix tomatoes with jalapeno, season, garlic, oregano, pepper, and salt and sprinkle the oil in a bowl, stir well, include them in your air fryer and cook for 15 min at 194 degs C.
2. Put tomatoes in a bowl, add parmesan and basil; stir and serve.

Nutrition: Calories 140; Fat 2 g; Carbohydrates 6 g; Sugar 2 g; Protein 8 g; Cholesterol 0 mg;

Air Fryer Fried Pickles

Prep T: 5 min | Cook T: 15 min | Servings: 4

Ingredients

- 64 grams crushed pork rinds
- 3 tbsp parmesan cheese, finely grated
- 16 sliced dill pickles
- 64 grams almond flour
- 1 large free-range egg, beaten
- 1 tsp olive oil

Directions

1. Preheat the air fryer to 187 degs C.
2. Mix the pork and parmesan properly in a shallow bowl.
3. Whisk eggs together properly in another bowl.
4. In another bowl, add the almond flour.
5. Dip the pickle in the almond flour, then the egg, then the pork and parmesan.
6. Cook for 6 min.
7. Serve and enjoy.

Nutrition: Calories: 245; Net carbs: 0g; Protein: 17g; Fat: 17g;

Crispy Prosciutto-Wrapped Asparagus

Prep T: 5 min | Cook T: 16 to 24 min | Servings: 6

Ingredients:

- 12 asparagus spears, woody ends trimmed
- 24 pieces thinly sliced prosciutto
- Cooking Spray

Directions:

1. Place the crisper tray on the air fry position. Select Air Fry, set the temperature to 182 degs C, and set the time to 4 min.
2. Wrap each asparagus spear with 2 slices of prosciutto, then repeat this process with the remaining asparagus and prosciutto.
3. Spray the crisper tray with cooking spray, then place 2 to 3 bundles in the crisper tray. Air fry for 4 min. Repeat this process with the remaining asparagus bundles.
4. Remove the bundles and allow to cool on a wire rack for 5 min before serving.

Nutrition: Calories 40; Fat 3 g; Carbohydrates 5g; Protein 12 g; Fiber 3 g; Sugar 2 g;

Garlic Sprouts

Prep T: 15 minutes | Cook T: 13 minutes | Servings: 6

Ingredients

- 453 grams of Brussels sprouts
- 1 tsp minced garlic
- 56 grams of celery stalks, minced
- 1 tbsp butter, melted
- 1 tsp cayenne pepper
- ¼ tsp salt

Directions

1. Chop the Brussels sprouts roughly and sprinkle with minced garlic, celery, cayenne pepper, salt, and butter. Shake well and leave for 10 minutes to marinate. Meanwhile, preheat the air fryer to 196 degs C. Put the marinated Brussels sprouts in the air fryer basket and cook them for 13 minutes.
2. Shake the vegetables from time to time during cooking.

Nutrition: Calories: 55; Fat: 2.3g; Fiber: 3.1g; Carbs: 8.1g; Protein:2.8g

Sausage Rolls

Prep T: 15 min | Cook T: 15 min | Servings: 12

Ingredients:

- 454 grams of bulk breakfast sausage
- 64 grams of finely chopped onion (about ½ medium onion)
- 1 garlic clove, minced or pressed
- ½ tsp dried sage (optional)
- ¼ tsp cayenne pepper
- ½ tsp dried mustard
- 1 large egg, beaten lightly
- 64 grams fresh bread crumbs
- 2 sheets (1 package) of frozen puff pastry, thawed
- All-purpose flour, for dusting

Directions:

1. In a medium bowl, break up the sausage. Add the onion, garlic, sage (if using), cayenne, mustard, egg, and bread crumbs. Mix to combine.
2. Divide the sausage mixture in half and tightly wrap each half in plastic wrap. Refrigerate for 5 to 10 min.
3. Lay out one of the pastry sheets on a lightly floured cutting board. Using a rolling pin, lightly roll out the pastry to smooth out the dough. Take out one of the sausage packages and form the sausage into a long roll (it's easiest to do this while the sausage is in the plastic wrap). Remove the plastic wrap and place the sausage on top of the puff pastry about 2.5 cm from one of the long edges. Roll the pastry around the sausage and pinch the edges of the dough together to seal.
4. Repeat with the other pastry sheet and sausage. Slice the logs into lengths about 4 cm long. (If you /have the time, freeze the logs for 10 min or so before slicing; it's much easier to slice.) Place the sausage rolls in the baking pan, cut-side down.
5. Place the pan on the roast position. Select Roast, set temperature to 177 degs C, and set time to 15 min.
6. After 7 or 8 min, rotate the pan 180 degs and continue cooking.
7. When cooking is complete, the rolls will be golden brown and sizzling. Remove the pan, let them cool for 5 min or so. If you like, serve them with honey mustard for dipping.

Nutrition: Calories 139; Fat 11 g; Carbohydrates 4 g; Protein 6 g; Fiber 0.3 g; Sugar 0.3 g;

Jicama Fries

Prep T: 31 min | Cook T: 10 min | Servings: 8

Ingredients

- 1 tbsp. dried thyme
- 96 grams arrowroot flour
- 1/2 large Jicama

- 2 eggs

Directions

1. Sliced jicama into fries.
2. Whisk eggs together and pour over fries. Toss to coat.
3. Mix a pinch of salt, thyme, and arrowroot flour together. Toss egg-coated jicama into dry mixture, tossing to coat well.
4. Cook 20 min on CHIPS setting. Toss halfway into the cooking process.

Nutrition: Calories 152; Fat 4 g; Carbohydrates 18 g; Sugar 0 g; Protein 4 g; Cholesterol 0 mg;

Spinach Salad

Prep T: 5 minutes | Cook T: 10 minutes | Servings: 4

Ingredients

- 453 grams of baby spinach
- Salt and black pepper to the taste
- 1 tbsp mustard
- Cooking Spray
- 32 grams apple cider vinegar
- 1 tbsp chives, chopped

Directions

1. Grease a pan that fits your air fryer with cooking spray, combine all the ingredients, introduce the pan in the fryer and cook at 176 degs C for 10 minutes.
2. Prepare the portions and serve them as a side dish.

Nutrition: Calories: 160; Fat: 3g; Fiber: 2g; Carbs: 4g; Protein:6g

Parsley Cauliflower Puree

Prep T: 10 minutes | Cook T: 8 minutes | Servings: 2

Ingredients

- 64 grams cauliflower, chopped
- 1 tbsp butter, melted
- ½ tsp salt
- 1 tbsp fresh parsley, chopped
- 32 grams heavy cream
- Cooking Spray

Directions

1. Put the cauliflower in the air fryer and spray with cooking spray. Cook it for 8 minutes at 205 degs C. Stir the vegetables after 4 minutes of cooking. Then preheat the heavy cream until it is hot and pour it in the blender.
2. Add cauliflower, parsley, salt, and butter. Blend the mixture until you get the smooth puree.

Nutrition: Calories: 122; Fat: 11.4g; Fiber: 1.9g; Carbs: 4.5g; Protein:1.9g

Kale Mash

Prep T: 5 minutes | Cook T: 20 minutes | Servings: 4

Ingredients

- 1 cauliflower head, florets separated
- 4 tsps butter, melted
- 4 garlic cloves, minced
- 384 grams of kale, chopped
- 2 scallions, chopped
- A pinch of salt and black pepper
- 42 grams of coconut cream
- tbsp parsley, chopped

Directions

1. In a pan that fits the air fryer, combine the cauliflower with the butter, garlic, scallions, salt, pepper and the cream, toss, introduce the pan in the machine and cook at 194 degs C for 20 minutes.
2. Mash the mix well, add the remaining ingredients, whisk, divide between plates and serve.

Nutrition: Calories: 198; Fat: 9g; Fiber: 2g; Carbs: 6g; Protein:8g

Green Celery Puree

Prep T: 10 minutes | Cook T: 6 minutes | Servings: 6

Ingredients

- 453 grams of celery stalks, chopped
- 64 grams spinach, chopped
- 56 grams of Parmesan, grated
- 32 grams chicken broth
- ½ tsp cayenne pepper

Directions

1. In the air fryer pan, mix celery stalk with chopped spinach, chicken broth, and cayenne pepper. Blend the mixture until homogenous. After this, top the puree with Parmesan. Preheat the air fryer to 205 degs C.
2. Put the pan with puree in the air fryer basket and cook the meal for 6 minutes.

Nutrition: Calories: 65; Fat: 2.4g; Fiber: 1.5g; Carbs: 7.5g; Protein:4.5g

Baked Potatoes

Prep T: 20 min | Cook T: 45 min | Servings: 6

Ingredients

- 6 potatoes
- 1 tbsp olive oil
- Salt to taste
- 128 grams butter
- 64 ml milk
- 64 grams sour cream
- 64 grams cheddar, shredded and divided

Directions

1. Poke the potatoes using a fork.

2. Add to the air fryer.
3. Set it to bake.
4. Cook at 204 degs C for 40 min.
5. Take out of the oven.
6. Slice the potato in half
7. Scoop out the potato flesh.
8. Mix potato flesh with the remaining ingredients.
9. Put the mixture back to the potato shells.
10. Bake in the air fryer for 5 min.

Serving Suggestions: Garnish with chopped green onions.

Prep & Cooking Tips: Use large Russet potatoes.

Nutrition: Calories 487; Fat 19 g; Carbohydrates 65 g; Protein 15 g; Fiber 7.5 g; Sugar 3 g;

Seafood Balls

Prep T: 15 min | Cook T: 15 min | Servings: 4
Ingredients

- 453 grams of salmon fillet, minced
- 1 egg, beaten
- 3 tbsp coconut, shredded
- 64 grams almond flour
- 1 tbsp avocado oil
- 1 tsp dried basil

Directions

1. In the mixing bowl, mix minced salmon fillet, egg, coconut, almond flour, and dried basil.
2. Make the balls from the fish mixture and put them in the air fryer basket.
3. Sprinkle the balls with avocado oil and cook at 185 degs C for 15 min.

Nutrition: Calories 268; Fat 16.4g; Fiber 2g; Carbs 3.9g; Protein 26.6g;

Golden Shrimp Toasts

Prep T: 15 min | Cook T: 8 min | Servings:: 4 to 6

Ingredients

- 227 grams of raw shrimp, peeled and deveined
- 1 egg, beaten
- 2 scallions, chopped, plus more for garnish
- 2 tbsp chopped fresh cilantro
- 2 tsps grated fresh ginger
- 1 to 2 tsps sriracha sauce
- 1 tsp soy sauce
- ½ tsp toasted sesame oil
- 6 slices thinly sliced white sandwich bread

- 64 grams sesame seeds
- Cooking Spray
- Thai chili sauce, for serving

Directions

1. In a food processor, add shrimp, egg, scallions, ginger, cilantro, sesame oil, soy sauce and sriracha sauce, and pulse until chopped finely. You'll eventually need to stop the food processor occasionally to scrape down the sides. Transfer the shrimp mixture to a bowl.
2. On a clean work surface, cut the crusts off the sandwich bread. Using a brush, generously brush one side of each slice of bread with shrimp mixture.
3. Place the sesame seeds on a plate. Press bread slices, shrimp-side down, into sesame seeds to coat evenly. Cut each slice diagonally into quarters.
4. Spritz the air fry basket with cooking spray. Spread the coated slices in a single layer in the air fry basket.
5. Place the basket on the air fry position.
6. Select Air Fry, set temperature to 205 degs C, and set time to 8 min. Flip the bread slices halfway through.
7. When cooking is complete, they should be golden and crispy. Remove from the air fryer grill to a plate and let cool for 5 min.

Nutrition: Calories 313; Fat 11 g; Carbohydrates 2 g; Protein 46 g; Fiber 0 g; Sugar 1 g;

Egg Cups

Prep T: 10 min | Cook T: 18 min | Servings: 12
Ingredients

- 12 eggs
- 114 grams of cream cheese
- 12 bacon strips, uncooked
- 32 grams buffalo sauce
- 85 grams cheddar cheese, shredded
- Pepper
- Salt

Directions

1. In a bowl, whisk together eggs, pepper, and salt.
2. Line each silicone muffin mold with one bacon strip.
3. Pour egg mixture into each muffin mold and place it in the air fryer basket. (In batches)
4. Cook at 176 degs C for 8 min.
5. In another bowl, mix cheddar cheese and cream cheese and microwave for 30 seconds. Add buffalo sauce and stir well.
6. Remove muffin molds from the air fryer and add 2 tsp. cheese mixture in the center of each egg cup.
7. Return muffin molds to the air fryer and cook for 10 min more.
8. Serve and enjoy.

Nutrition: Calories 225; Fat 15 g; Carbohydrates 1 g; Sugar 0 g; Protein 11 g; Cholesterol 0 mg;

Turmeric Cauliflower Rice

Prep T: 5 minutes | Cook T: 20 minutes | Servings: 4
Ingredients

- 1 big cauliflower, florets separated and riced
- 192 ml chicken stock
- 1 tbsp olive oil
- Salt and black pepper to the taste
- ½ tsp turmeric powder

Directions

1. In a pan that fits the air fryer, combine the cauliflower with the oil and the rest of the ingredients, toss, introduce in the air fryer and cook at 183 degs C for 20 minutes.
2. Prepare the portions and serve them as a side dish.

Nutrition: Calories: 193; Fat: 5g; Fiber: 2g; Carbs: 4g; Protein:6g

Basil Tomatoes

Prep T: 5 minutes | Cook T: 15 minutes | Servings: 4

Ingredients

- 4 tomatoes, halved
- ½ tsp smoked paprika
- ½ tsp garlic powder
- ½ tsp onion powder
- ½ tsp oregano, dried
- 1 tbsp basil, chopped
- 64 grams parmesan, grated
- Cooking Spray

Directions

1. In a bowl, mix all the ingredients except the cooking spray and the parmesan. Arrange the tomatoes in your air fryer's pan, sprinkle the parmesan on top and grease with cooking spray.
2. Cook at 188 degs C for 15 minutes, divide between plates and serve.

Nutrition: Calories: 200; Fat: 7g; Fiber: 2g; Carbs: 4g; Protein:6g

Artichokes Sauté

Prep T: 5 minutes | Cook T: 15 minutes | Servings: 4

Ingredients

- 283 grams of artichoke hearts, halved
- 3 garlic cloves
- 256 grams baby spinach
- 32 grams veggie stock
- 2 tsps lime juice
- Salt and black pepper to the taste

Directions

1. In a pan suitable for your air fryer, mix all the ingredients, toss, introduce in the fryer and cook at 187 degs C for 15 minutes.
2. Prepare the portions and serve them as a side dish.

Nutrition: Calories: 209; Fat: 6g; Fiber: 2g; Carbs: 4g; Protein:8g

Golden Asparagus Frittata

Prep T: 5 min | Cook T: 25 min | Servings: 2 to 4

Ingredients:

- 128 grams asparagus spears, cut into 2.5 cm pieces
- 1 tsp vegetable oil
- 1 tbsp milk
- 6 eggs, beaten
- 57 grams of goat cheese, crumbled
- 1 tbsp minced chives, optional
- Kosher salt and pepper, to taste

Directions:

1. Add the asparagus spears to a small bowl and drizzle with the vegetable oil. Toss until well coated and transfer to the air fry basket.
2. Place the basket on the air fry position.
3. Select Air Fry. Set temperature to 205 degs C and set time to 5 min. Flip the asparagus halfway through.
4. When cooking is complete, the asparagus should be tender and slightly wilted.
5. Remove the asparagus from the air fryer grill to a baking pan.
6. Stir together the milk and eggs in a medium bowl. Pour the mixture over the asparagus in the pan. Sprinkle with the goat cheese and the chives (if using) over the eggs. Season with salt and pepper.
7. Place the pan on the bake position.
8. Select Bake, set temperature to 160 degs C and set time to 20 min.
9. When cooking is complete, the top should be golden and the eggs should be set.
10. Transfer to a serving dish. Slice and serve.

Nutrition: Calories 370; Fat 25 g; Carbohydrates 4 g; Sugar 0.6 g; Protein 27 g; Fiber 1 g;

Delicious Potato Frittata

Prep T: 10 min | Cook T: 20 min | Servings: 6

Ingredients

- 170 grams of jarred roasted red bell peppers, chopped
- 12 eggs, whisked
- 64 grams parmesan, grated
- 3 garlic cloves, minced
- 2 tbsp parsley, chopped
- Salt and black pepper to the taste
- 2 tbsp chives, chopped
- 16 potato wedges
- 6 tbsp ricotta cheese
- Cooking Spray

Directions

1. In a bowl, mix eggs with red peppers, garlic, parsley, salt, pepper and ricotta and whisk well.
2. Heat up your air fryer at 150 degs C and grease it with cooking spray.
3. Add half of the potato wedges on the bottom and sprinkle half of the parmesan all over.
4. Add half of the egg mix; add the rest of the potatoes and the rest of the parmesan.
5. Add the rest of the eggs mix, sprinkle chives and cook for 20 min.
6. Divide among plates and serve for breakfast.
7. Enjoy!

Nutrition: Calories 312; Fat 6; Fiber 9; Carbs 16; Protein 5

Chapter 3: Bread and Pizza

Garlic Bread

Prep T: 10 minutes | Cook T: 8 minutes | Servings: 4

Ingredients

- 30 grams of Mozzarella, shredded
- 2 tbsp almond flour
- 1 tsp cream cheese
- ¼ tsp garlic powder
- ¼ tsp baking powder
- 1 egg, beaten
- 1 tsp coconut oil, melted
- ¼ tsp minced garlic
- 1 tsp dried dill
- 30 grams of Provolone cheese, grated

Directions

1. In the mixing bowl mix up Mozzarella, almond flour, cream cheese, garlic powder, baking powder, egg, minced garlic, dried dill, and Provolone cheese. When the mixture is homogenous, transfer it on the baking paper and spread it in the shape of the bread. Sprinkle the garlic bread with coconut oil.
2. Preheat the air fryer to 205 degs C. Transfer the baking paper with garlic bread in the air fryer and cook for 8 minutes or until it is light brown.
3. When the garlic bread is cooked, cut it on 4 servings and place it in the serving plates.

Nutrition: Calories: 155; Fat: 12.7g; Fiber: 1.6g; Carbs: 4g; Protein:8.3g

Mushroom and Spinach Calzones

Prep T: 15 min | Cook T: 26 to 27 min | Servings: 4

Ingredients

- 2 tbsp olive oil
- 1 onion, chopped
- 2 garlic cloves, minced
- 32 grams chopped mushrooms
- 454 grams of spinach, chopped
- 1 tbsp Italian seasoning
- 1/2 tsp oregano
- Salt and black pepper, to taste
- 192 grams marinara sauce
- 128 grams ricotta cheese, crumbled
- 369 grams of pizza crust
- Cooking Spray

Directions

Make the Filling:

1. Heat the olive oil in a pan over medium heat until shimmering.
2. Add the onion, garlic, and mushrooms and sauté for 4 min, or until softened.
3. Stir in the spinach and sauté for 2 to 3 min, or until the spinach is wilted. Sprinkle with the Italian seasoning, oregano, salt, and pepper and mix well.
4. Add the marinara sauce and cook for about 5 min, stirring occasionally, or until the sauce is thickened.

5. Remove the pan from the heat and stir in the ricotta cheese. Set aside.

Make the Calzones:

1. Spritz the crisper tray with cooking spray.
2. Place the crisper tray on the air fry position. Select Air Fry, set the temperature to 191 degs C and set the time to 15 min.
3. Roll the pizza crust out with a rolling pin on a lightly floured work surface, then cut it into 4 rectangles.
4. Spoon 1/4 of the filling into each rectangle and fold in half. Crimp the edges with a fork to seal. Mist them with cooking spray.
5. Place the calzones in the crisper tray. Air fry for 15 min, flipping once, or until the calzones are golden brown and crisp.
6. Transfer the calzones to a paper towel-lined plate and serve.

Nutrition: Calories 314; Fat 16 g; Carbohydrates 32 g; Protein 11.3 g; Fiber 4 g; Sugar 7.5 g;

Greek Bread

Prep T: 15 minutes | Cook T: 4 minutes | Servings: 6

Ingredients

- 128 grams Mozzarella, shredded
- 2 tbsp Greek yogurt
- 1 egg, beaten
- ½ tsp baking powder
- 64 grams almond flour
- 1 tsp butter, melted

Directions

1. In the glass bowl mix up Mozzarella and yogurt. Microwave the mixture for 2 minutes. After this, mix up baking powder, almond flour, and egg. Combine together the almond flour mixture and melted Mozzarella mixture.
2. Stir it with the help of the spatula until smooth. Refrigerate the dough for 10 minutes. Then cut it on 6 pieces and roll up to get the flatbread pieces.
3. Air fryer the bread for 3 minutes at 205 degs C. Then brush it with melted butter and cook for 1 minute more or until the bread is light brown.

Nutrition: Calories: 43; Fat: 3.4g; Fiber: 0.3g; Carbs: 0.9g; Protein:2.8g

Cheesy Apple Roll-Ups

Prep T: 5 min | Cook T: 4 to 5 min | Makes 8 roll-ups

Ingredients:

- 8 slices whole wheat sandwich bread
- 113 grams of Colby Jack cheese, grated
- ½ small apple, chopped
- 2 tbsp butter, melted

Directions:

1. Place the crisper tray on the air fry position. Select Air Fry, set the temperature to 199 degs C, and set the time to 5 min.
2. Remove the crusts from the bread and flatten the slices with a rolling pin. Don't be gentle. Press hard so that bread will be very thin.
3. Top bread slices with cheese and chopped apple, dividing the ingredients evenly.
4. Roll up each slice tightly and secure each with one or two toothpicks.
5. Brush outside of rolls with melted butter.
6. Place in the crisper tray. Air fry for 4 to 5 min, or until outside is crisp and nicely browned.
7. Serve hot.

Nutrition: Calories: 81; Fat 7 g; Carbohydrates 4 g; Protein 3 g; Fiber 0.2 g; Sugar 1.5 g;

Vegan Corn Bread

Prep T: 10 min | Cook T: 10 min | Servings: 9

Ingredients

- 50 grams of all-purpose flour
- 80 ml of applesauce
- 300 ml of almond milk
- 1 tablespoon of baking powder
- 80 grams of sugar
- 230 gr of yellow corn flour
- 1 teaspoon of salt

Directions

1. In a bowl mix flour, cornmeal, sugar, yeast and salt
2. Stir in the milk and applesauce and then mix everything well.
3. Pour the batter into the silicone muffin cups.
4. Place the baking cups in the air fryer's basket and cook at 200 degs C for 8-10 min.
5. Serve and enjoy your meal!

Nutrition: Calories: 132; Fat: 2 g; Protein: 2 g; Carbs: 28 g; Fiber: 1.6 g; Sugar: 13 g

Banana Bread

Prep T: 10 min | Cook T: 35 min | Servings: 10

Ingredients

- 2 eggs, lightly beaten
- 150 grams of all-purpose flour
- 1 teaspoon of vanilla
- 60 grams of butter, melted
- 230 g of mashed banana
- 1/4 teaspoon of baking soda
- 1/2 teaspoon of baking powder
- 70 grams of sugar
- 1/4 teaspoon of salt

Directions

1. Preheat the air fryer to 160 degs C.

2. Mix the flour, baking soda, baking powder, sugar, and salt in a bowl.
3. In a separate bowl, beat the eggs with the vanilla, butter and bananas until well combined.
4. Add the flour mixture to the egg mixture and stir until everything is well combined.
5. Pour the batter into the greased pan of the air fryer.
6. Place the pan in the basket of the air fryer and cook for 35 min
7. Slice and serve.

Nutrition: Calories: 161; Fat: 6 g; Protein: 3 g; Carbs: 24 g; Fiber: 1.9 g; Sugar: 10 g

Bread with apples and courgettes

Prep T: 10 min | Cook T: 30 min | Servings: 10

Ingredients

- 1 egg
- 150 grams of multi-purpose flour
- 50 grams of walnuts, chopped
- 100 grams of chopped zucchini
- 120 grams of chopped apples
- 1 teaspoon of vanilla
- 50 ml of vegetable oil
- 1/4 teaspoon of baking soda
- 3/4 teaspoon of baking powder
- 1 1/4 teaspoon of cinnamon
- 1/4 teaspoon of salt

Directions

1. Preheat the air fryer to 160 degs C.
2. Mix the flour, baking soda, baking powder, cinnamon, and salt in a bowl.
3. In a separate bowl, beat the egg with the vanilla, oil and sugar until well blended.
4. Incorporate the flour mixture into the egg mixture and mix until everything is well combined. Add the zucchini, walnuts and apple and mix.
5. Pour the batter into the greased pan of the air fryer.
6. Place it in the air fryer's basket and cook for 30 min.
7. Slice and serve.

Nutrition: Calories: 119; Fat: 6 g; Protein: 3.5 g; Carbs: 12 g; Fiber: 2.2 g; Sugar: 1.2 g

Zucchini Bread

Prep T: 10 min | Cook T: 25 min | Servings: 6

Ingredients

- 1 egg
- 250 grams of almond flour
- 80 grams of butter, melted
- 120 ml of sugar-free almond milk
- 120 gr of Erythritol
- 120 grams of coconut flour
- 150 grams of chopped zucchini, squeezed
- 1 teaspoon of baking soda
- 1 teaspoon of cinnamon
- 2 teaspoons of lemon juice
- 1/8 teaspoon of salt

Directions

1. In a bowl, mix the almond flour with cinnamon, baking soda, coconut flour, erythritol and salt.
2. Beat the egg with milk, butter, lemon juice and zucchini in another bowl.
3. Add the egg mixture to the almond flour mixture and mix until well blended.
4. Pour the batter into the greased pan for the air fryer.
5. Place the pan in the air fryer's basket and cook at 160 degs C for 25 min.
6. Slice and serve.

Nutrition: Calories: 326; Fat: 12 g; Protein: 32 g; Carbs: 12 g; Fiber: 0.2 g; Sugar: 2.5 g

Wet Banana Bread

Prep T: 10 min | Cook T: 30 min | Servings: 4
Ingredients

- 1 egg
- 1/2 teaspoon of baking soda
- 60 ml of sour cream
- 2 tablespoons of butter, melted
- 3 tablespoons of brown sugar
- 100 grams of all-purpose flour
- 1 ripe banana, mashed
- 1/4 teaspoon of salt

Directions

1. Preheat the air fryer to 160 degs C.
2. Combine the egg, banana, brown sugar, butter, and sour cream in a bowl.
3. Incorporate the flour with baking soda and salt and beat everything well.
4. Pour the mixture into the greased pan for the air fryer.
5. Insert the pan into the air fryer's basket and cook for 25-30 min.
6. Slice and serve.

Nutrition: Calories: 182; Fat: 9 g; Protein: 5 g; Carbs: 20.5 g; Fiber: 2.5 g; Sugar: 2 g

Banana Bread with Chocolate Chips

Prep T: 10 min | Cook T: 20 min | Servings: 6
Ingredients

- 3 eggs
- 100 grams of mashed banana
- 180 grams of chocolate chips
- 1 tablespoon of vanilla
- 245 ml of milk
- 6 tablespoons of butter, soft
- 1/2 teaspoon of baking soda
- 1/2 teaspoon of baking powder
- 150 grams of sugar
- 250 grams of flour
- 1/2 teaspoon of salt

Directions

1. In a bowl, beat the butter and sugar until light and fluffy.

2. Add vanilla and eggs and mix everything well.
3. Add flour, baking soda, baking powder, and salt and mix to combine.
4. Add the mashed banana and milk and knead well. Add the chocolate chips and mix everything.
5. Pour the batter into the greased pan for the air fryer.
6. Put the dough in the air fryer's basket and cook at 180 degs C for 20 min.
7. Slice and serve.

Nutrition: Calories: 583; Fat: 27 g; Protein: 11.5 g; Carbs: 75 g; Fiber: 7 g; Sugar: 38 g

Cauliflower Bread

Preparation: 25 Minutes | Cooking Time: 25 Minutes | Servings: 4
Ingredients

- 500 grams of almond flour
- 2 eggs, beaten
- 1 tablespoon of flax seeds
- 240 grams cauliflower florets, grated
- 120 ml of buttermilk
- 6 tablespoons of butter, melted
- Salt to taste.

Directions

1. Preheat the air fryer to 175 degs C for 5 min.
2. Line a mold with baking paper.
3. In a bowl, beat the eggs, add the buttermilk, flour, butter, salt, and mix thoroughly.
4. Add the cauliflower florets and flax seeds.
5. Mix well.
6. Pour the mixture into the already greased mold.
7. Insert into the air fryer.
8. Bake for 20-25 min at 160 degs C.
9. When ready, serve and enjoy.

Nutrition: Calories: 700; Fat: 20 g; Protein: 74 g; Carbs: 61 g; Fiber: 1 g; Sugar: 15.5 g

Banana and Raisin Bread

Preparation: 22 Minutes | Cooking Time: 40 Minutes | Servings: 4
Ingredients

- 500 grams of almond flour
- 1 teaspoon of baking powder
- A pinch of salt
- 4 large bananas, ripe and peeled
- 120 grams of brown sugar
- 3 large eggs
- 4 tablespoons of Greek yogurt
- 2 tablespoons of peanut butter
- 1 teaspoon of vanilla extract
- 120 grams of raisins
- Spray oil, for greasing

Directions

1. Preheat the air fryer to 175 degs C for 5 min.
2. Line a pan with parchment paper.
3. Put the flour, baking powder, salt and sugar in a bowl.
4. Whisk the eggs in a separate bowl and add the butter, vanilla extract and yogurt

5. Mix well and then mix in the ingredients from both bowls.
6. Add raisins and mashed bananas.
7. Mix very well.
8. Pour this batter into an already greased mold.
9. Place in the air fryer and cook for 40 min at 140 degs C.
10. When ready, serve and enjoy.

Nutrition: Calories: 700; Fat: 9 g; Protein: 70 g; Carbs: 94 g; Fiber: 2 g; Sugar: 39 g

Cranberry Bread

Preparation: 15 Minutes | Cooking Time: 25 Minutes | Servings: 2
Ingredients

- 350 grams of almond flour
- 60 ml of melted butter
- 120 ml almond milk
- 1 teaspoon of vanilla extract
- 4 tablespoons of brown sugar
- 80 grams of blueberries
- 1 teaspoon of dry yeast, dissolved in 2 tablespoons of warm water
- A pinch of salt
- Spray oil, for greasing

Directions

1. Take a large bowl and add the melted butter, vanilla extract and yeast water.
2. Add a pinch of salt and sugar.
3. Now, add flour and almond milk
4. Combine all the ingredients to form a dough.
5. Incorporate the blueberries at the end.
6. Pour the mixture into the already oiled mold.
7. Place the pan in the air fryer.
8. Set the timer to 25 min for 200 degs C.
9. Once the bread is cooked, take it out of the oven and serve.

Nutrition: Calories: 875; Fat: 22 g; Protein: 87 g; Carbs: 85 g; Fiber: 0.5 g; Sugar: 20 g

French pizza

Prep T: 10 min | Cook T: 8 min | Servings: 4
Ingredients

- 1 French loaf of bread, cut in half lengthwise

- 240 grams mozzarella, chopped
- 240 ml of pizza sauce
- 8 basil leaves
- 45 grams olives, sliced

Directions

1. Preheat the air fryer to 180 degs C.
2. Spread the pizza sauce on one side of the loaf and coat it with cheese, basil, and olives.
3. Place the bread slices in the air fryer's basket and cook for 5-8 min.
4. Serve and enjoy your meal!

Nutrition: Calories: 382; Fat: 15 g; Protein: 21 g; Carbs: 39 g; Fiber: 2.2 g; Sugar: 5.5 g

Peppers pizza

Prep T: 10 min | Cook T: 8 min | Servings: 1
Ingredients

- 1 whole wheat pita
- 8 sliced peppers
- 2 tablespoons of cheddar, chopped
- 2 tablespoons of mozzarella, chopped
- 2 tablespoons of pizza sauce

Directions

1. Sprinkle the pizza sauce over the pita and then place the pepperoni slices, cheddar and mozzarella on top.
2. Grease the pizza with cooking spray, place it in the air fryer's basket, and cook at 200 degs C for 8 min.
3. Remove the pizza from the air fryer basket and allow it to cool.
4. Serve and enjoy your meal!

Nutrition: Calories: 676; Fat: 15 g; Protein: 26 g; Carbs: 112 g; Fiber: 16 g; Sugar: 37 g

Chapter 4: Vegetables and Vegetarian

Tofu Nuggets

Prep T: 15 min | Cook T: 25 min | Servings: 4

Ingredients

Tofu:

- 396 grams of tofu, sliced into cubes
- Cooking Spray
- 32 grams flour
- 1 tsp garlic powder
- 1/2 tsp paprika
- 1/2 tsp ground cumin
- Salt to taste

Sauce:

- 1 tbsp avocado oil
- 2 tbsp sugar
- 3 tbsp soy sauce
- 2 tbsp honey
- 1 tsp garlic powder
- 1 tbsp ginger, grated
- Pepper to taste

Directions

1. Spray tofu cubes with oil.
2. Mix remaining ingredients in a bowl.
3. Coat tofu evenly with this mixture.
4. Add the tofu cubes to the air fryer.
5. Set it to air fry.
6. Cook at 177 degs C for 10 min.
7. Toss and cook for 15 min.
8. In a bowl, mix the sauce ingredients.
9. Toss the tofu in the sauce and serve.

Serving Suggestions: Garnish with sesame seeds and chopped chives.

Prep & Cooking Tips: Use maple syrup if honey is not available.

Nutrition: Calories 140; Fat 8.25 g; Carbohydrates 8 g; Protein 10 g; Fiber 0.4 g; Sugar 12 g;

Asparagus Salad with Boiled Eggs

Prep T: 35 min | Cook T: 20 min |Serving: 4

Ingredients

- 32 grams olive oil
- 453 grams of asparagus, trimmed
- 128 grams cherry tomatoes, halved
- 32 grams balsamic vinegar
- 1 garlic cloves, minced
- 2 scallion stalks, chopped
- 1/2 tsp oregano
- Coarse sea salt and ground black pepper, to your liking
- 2 hard-boiled eggs, sliced

Directions

1. Start by preheating your Air Fryer to 105 degs C. Brush the cooking basket with 1 tbsp of olive oil.
2. Add the asparagus and cherry tomatoes to the cooking basket. Drizzle 1 tbsp of olive oil all over your veggies.
3. Cook for 5 min, shaking the basket halfway through the cooking time. Let it cool slightly.
4. Toss with the remaining olive oil, balsamic vinegar, garlic, scallions, oregano, salt, and black pepper.
5. Afterwards, add the hard-boiled eggs on the top of your salad and serve.

Nutrition: Calories: 143; Fat: 11 g; Protein: 6 g; Carbs: 10g; Net Carbs: 6.5 g; Fiber: 2g; Sugar: 4 g

Spicy creamed mushrooms

Prep T: 5 min | Cook T: 8 min | Servings: 4

Ingredients

- 1 Butter Teaspoon
- 1 Onion, Sliced
- 128 grams of Ice with Cream
- 255 grams of White mushrooms
- 1 Red Pepper Teaspoon, Chili Flakes, Garlic

Directions

1. Start by slicing your mushrooms, and then add red pepper and chili flakes to the sprinkles. Make sure you're mixing properly, and then pre-heat the air fryer to 204 degs C.
2. Oil the basket of the air fryer with olive oil and add to your mushrooms. Cook for five min, and then add the rest of your ingredients. Lower the temperature to 185 degs C, and cook for another seven min. Before eating, stir well.

Nutrition: Calories 123; Fat 1 g; Carbohydrates 8 g; Sugar 8 g; Protein 1 g; Cholesterol 0 mg;

Air Fryer Falafel

Prep T: 40 min | Cook T: 23 min | Servings: 6

Ingredients

- 1 drained 425 grams can of chickpeas
- 128 grams white onion chopped
- 6 small garlic cloves
- 1 tbsp of juice from a lemon
- 128 grams of thinly packed leaves with parsley
- 64 grams of thinly packed coriander leaves
- 32 grams of thinly packed fresh leaves of dill
- 1 tsp powder for baking
- 2 cumin tsps

- 1 salt tsp
- 64 grams of flour (either all-purpose flour or 1:1 gluten-free flour)

For the Tahini Sauce for Vegan Yogurt:
- 128 grams of plain yogurt vegan (not vanilla flavored)
- Tahini 1 tbsp
- Lemon juice, 2 tsps

Directions

1. Fill the food processor with chickpeas, onion, garlic, lemon juice, parsley, cilantro, dill, flour, baking powder, cumin, and salt. Pulse until it forms a coarse crumb texture. Stop scraping down the bowl's sides as needed.
2. Transfer to a bowl then cover, and refrigerate the falafel mixture for 1 hour (or up to 2 days before cooking).
3. Prepare the vegan tahini sauce as the falafel mixture sets. Whisk the vegan yogurt, tahini, and lemon juice together until mixed. To mix, add salt and pepper and stir. Cover until time to eat, and then refrigerate.
4. Using a spoon or cookie dough scooper to measure out 1 tbsp of the dough until the falafel mixture is cooled. Shape yourself into balls. Place the balls of falafel on a tray. Repeat until they have used all the batter.
5. Spray with vegetable cooking spray on the air fryer basket. Preheat the fryer to 190 degs C.
6. Place the raw falafel in the basket using tongs, arranging them on the bottom of the basket. Set the basket to the air fryer and then cook for 15 min, removing the basket and turning the falafel once or twice with the tongs during cooking time. When done, remove the falafel from the basket of an air fryer. Enable them slightly to cool.
7. Put falafel on a tray to serve and serve for dipping with tahini sauce. Or add 3-4 falafels along with hummus, chopped romaine lettuce, and chopped onions within a halved pita. Drizzle the tahini sauce with it.

Nutrition: Calories 214; Fat 1 g; Carbohydrates 14 g; Sugar 2 g; Protein 21 g; Cholesterol 0 mg;

Cherry Tomatoes Skewers

Prep T: 10 min | Cook T: 26 min | Servings: 4

Ingredients

- 3 tbsp. balsamic vinegar
- 24 cherry tomatoes
- 2 tbsp. olive oil
- Three garlic cloves
- 1 tbsp. thyme
- Salt and black pepper

For dressing:
- 2 tbsp. balsamic vinegar
- Salt and black pepper
- 4 tbsp. olive oil

Directions

1. Mix in 2 tbsp. vinegar with three tbsp. oil, three garlic cloves, black pepper, and thyme, salt in a bowl and beat properly.
2. Put tomatoes. Toss to coat and allow for 30 min.
3. Assemble six tomatoes on one skewer. Do the same with the remaining tomatoes.
4. Put into an air fryer and cook at 182 degs C for 6 min.
5. Mix in 2 tbsp. vinegar with salt, four tbsp. oil and pepper. Beat properly.
6. Assemble tomato skewers on plates.
7. Serve with dressing sprinkled over.

Nutrition: Calories: 210; Protein: 0.61 g; Fat: 20.34 g; Carbohydrates: 6.53 g;

Bean and Corn Stuffed Peppers

Prep T: 15 min | Cook T: 32 min | Servings: 6

Ingredients

- 6 red or green bell peppers, seeded, ribs removed, and top 1.5 cm cut off and reserved
- 4 garlic cloves, minced
- 1 small white onion, diced
- 482 grams bags instant rice, cooked in microwave
- 284 grams can red or green enchilada sauce
- 1/2 tsp chili powder
- 1/4 tsp ground cumin
- 64 grams canned black beans, rinsed and drained
- 64 grams frozen corn
- 64 grams vegetable stock
- 227 grams bag shredded Colby Jack cheese, divided

Directions

1. Chop the 1.2 cm portions of reserved bell pepper and place in a large mixing bowl. Add the garlic, onion, cooked instant rice, enchilada sauce, chili powder, cumin, black beans, corn, vegetable stock, and half the cheese. Mix to combine.
2. Place the baking pan on the roast position. Select Roast, set the temperature to 177 degs C, and set the time to 32 min.
3. Spoon the mixture into the peppers, filling them up as full as possible. If necessary, lightly press the mixture down into the peppers to fit more in.
4. Place the peppers, upright, in the pan. Roast for 30 min.
5. After 30 min, sprinkle the remaining cheese over the top of the peppers. Roast for the remaining 2 min.
6. When cooking is complete, serve immediately.

Nutrition: Calories 397; Fat 3 g; Carbohydrates 80 g; Protein 10.5 g; Fiber 7.5 g; Sugar 5.3 g;

Vegetarian Meatballs

Prep T: 15 min | Cook T: 18 min | Servings: 3

Ingredients

- 64 grams grated carrots
- 64 grams sweet onions
- 2 tbsp olive oil
- 128 grams rolled oats
- 64 grams roasted cashews
- 256 grams cooked chickpeas
- Juice of 1 lemon
- 2 tbsp soy sauce
- 1 tbsp flax meal
- 1 tsp garlic powder
- 1 tsp cumin
- 1/2 tsp turmeric

Directions

1. Place the baking pan on the roast position. Select Roast, set the temperature to 177 degs C, and set the time to 6 min.
2. Mix together the carrots, onions, and olive oil in the pan and stir to combine.
3. Roast for 6 min.
4. Meanwhile, put the oats and cashews in a food processor or blender and pulse until coarsely ground. Transfer the mixture to a large bowl. Add the chickpeas, lemon juice, and soy sauce to the food processor and pulse until smooth. Transfer the chickpea mixture to the bowl of oat and cashew mixture.
5. Remove the carrots and onions from the pan to the bowl of chickpea mixture. Add the flax meal, garlic powder, cumin, turmeric, and stir to incorporate.
6. Scoop tbsp-sized portions of the veggie mixture and roll them into balls with your hands. Transfer the balls to the crisper tray in a single layer.
7. Increase the temperature to 188 degs C and bake for 12 min until golden through. Flip the balls halfway through the cooking time.
8. Serve warm.

Nutrition: Calories 573; Fat 12 g; Carbohydrates 90 g; Protein 27 g; Fiber 17 g; Sugar 17.5 g;

Tasty Squash Stew

Prep T: 10 min | Cook T: 30 min | Servings: 8

Ingredients

- 2 carrots, chopped
- 1 yellow onion, chopped
- 2 celery stalks, chopped
- 2 green apples, cored, peeled and chopped
- 4 garlic cloves, minced
- 256 grams butternut squash, peeled and cubed
- 170 grams of canned chickpeas, drained
- 170 grams of canned black beans, drained
- 200 grams of canned coconut milk
- 2 tsp. chili powder
- 1 tsp. oregano, dried
- 1 tbsp. cumin , ground
- 256 ml veggie stock
- 2 tbsp. tomato paste
- Salt and black pepper to taste
- 1 tbsp. cilantro, chopped

Directions

1. In your air fryer, mix carrots with onion, celery, apples, garlic, squash, chickpeas, black beans, coconut milk, chili powder, oregano, cumin , stock, tomato paste, salt and pepper.
2. Stir, cover and cook at 188 degs C for 30 min

3. Add cilantro and stir.
4. Divide into bowls and serve hot.

Nutrition: Calories: 112; Protein: 3.28 g; Fat: 2.37 g; Carbohydrates: 21.99 g;

Spinach and Zucchini Rolls

Prep T: 15 min | Cook T: 18 min | Servings: 6

Ingredients

- 3 large zucchinis
- 2 1/2 tsps kosher salt or 1 1/4 tsps fine salt, divided
- 164 gramss cooked chopped spinach
- 164 gramss whole milk ricotta cheese
- 64 grams freshly grated Parmesan cheese
- 164 gramss shredded Mozzarella, divided
- 1 large egg, lightly beaten
- 1 tsp Italian seasoning or 1/2 tsp each dried basil and oregano
- Freshly ground black pepper
- Cooking oil spray
- 164 gramss Marinara Sauce or store-bought variety

Directions

1. Cut off the zucchini ends and peel several strips off one side to make a flat base. Use a large Y-shaped peeler or sharp cheese plane to cut long slices about 2.5 cm thick. When you get to a point where you can't get any more slices, set that zucchini aside and start on the next. You need 8 good slices per squash, for a total of 24 slices (a few extra never hurts). Save the rest of the zucchini pieces for another recipes.
2. Salt one side of the zucchini slices with 1 tsp of kosher salt. Place the slices salted-side down on a rack placed over a baking sheet. Salt the other sides with another tsp of kosher salt. Let the slices sit for 10 min, or until they start to exude water (you'll see it beading up on the surface of the slices and dripping onto the baking sheet).
3. While the zucchini sits, in a medium bowl, combine the spinach, ricotta, Parmesan cheese, 96 grams of Mozzarella, egg, Italian seasoning, remaining 1/2 tsp of kosher salt, and pepper.
4. Spray the baking pan with cooking oil spray.
5. Rinse the zucchini slices off and blot them dry with a paper towel. Spread about 2 tbsp of the ricotta mixture evenly along each zucchini slice. Roll up the slice and place each seam-side down on the prepared baking pan. Place the rolls so they touch, working from the center of the pan out toward the edges. Repeat with remaining zucchini slices and filling. Top the rolls with the marinara sauce and sprinkle with the remaining96 grams of Mozzarella.
6. Place the pan on the roast position. Select Roast, set temperature to 191 degs C, and set time to 18 min.

7. After about 15 min, check the rolls. They are done when the cheese is melted and beginning to brown, and the filling is bubbling. If necessary, continue cooking for another 3 to 4 min.
8. When cooking is complete, remove the pan from the grill. Serve.

Nutrition: Calories 305; Fat 21 g; Carbohydrates 8 g; Protein 20 g; Fiber 1 g; Sugar 2.5 g;

Golden Cabbage and Mushroom Spring Rolls

Prep T: 20 min | Cook T: 14 min | Makes 14 spring rolls

Ingredients

- 2 tbsp vegetable oil
- 512 grams sliced Napa cabbage
- 142 grams of shiitake mushrooms, diced
- 3 carrots, cut into thin matchsticks
- 1 tbsp minced fresh ginger
- 1 tbsp minced garlic
- 1 bunch scallions, only white and light green parts, sliced
- 2 tbsp soy sauce
- 113 grams of package cellophane noodles
- 1/4 tsp cornstarch
- 340 grams of package frozen spring roll wrappers, thawed
- Cooking Spray

Directions

1. Warm up the olive oil in a nonstick skillet over medium-high heat until shimmering.
2. Add the cabbage, carrots, mushrooms, and sauté for 3 min or until tender.
3. Add the garlic, scallions, and ginger and sauté for 1 minute or until fragrant.
4. Mix in the soy sauce and turn off the heat. Discard any liquid that remains in the skillet and allow it to cool for a few min.
5. Bring a pot of water to a boil, then turn off the heat and pour in the noodles. Let sit for 10 min or until the noodles are al dente. Transfer 128 grams of the noodles to the skillet and toss with the cooked vegetables. Reserve the remaining noodles for other use.
6. Dissolve the cornstarch in a small water dish, then place the wrappers on a clean work surface. Dab the edges of the wrappers with cornstarch.
7. Scoop up 3 tbsp of filling in the center of each wrapper, then fold the corner in front of you over the filling. Tuck the wrapper under the filling, then fold the corners on both sides into the center. Keep rolling to seal the wrapper. Repeat with remaining wrappers.
8. Spritz the air fry basket with cooking spray. Arrange the wrappers in the basket and spritz them with cooking spray.

9. Place the basket on the air fry position.
10. Select Air Fry, set temperature to 205 degs C, and set time to 10 min. Flip the wrappers halfway through the cooking time.
11. When cooking is complete, the wrappers will be golden brown.
12. Serve immediately.

Nutrition: Calories 159; Fat 1.5 g; Carbohydrates 28 g; Protein 10 g; Fiber 7 g; Sugar 2 g;

Toasted-Baked Tofu cubes

Prep T and Cook T: 30 min | Servings: 2

Ingredients

- 1/2 block of tofu, cubed
- 1 tbsp. olive oil
- 1 tbsp. Nutritional yeast
- 1 tbsp. flour
- 1/4 tsp. black pepper
- 1 tsp. sea salt
- 1/2 tsp. garlic powder

Directions

1. Combine all the ingredients with tofu
2. Preheat the Air Fryer at 230 degs C.
3. Bake tofu on a lined baking tray for 15-30 min, turn it around every 10 min.

Nutrition: Calories 158; Fat 13 g; Carbohydrates 5 g; Protein 1 g; Fiber 0 g; Sugar 0 g;

Spinach Quiche

Prep T: 10 min | Cook T: 15 min | Servings: 6

Ingredients

- 64 grams of Flour Almond
- 128 grams of Spinach
- 32 grams of Cream Cheese
- 170 grams of Cheddar Cheese, Shredded
- 3 Eggs

Directions

1. Combine the almond flour with 4 tbsp. In salt and water. Mix until the soft dough is formed. This ought not to be sticky.
2. Spray the olive oil on your air fryer and pre-heat it to 190 degs C.
3. Put your dough in your air fryer and roll it out. It ought to be in the form of a crust.
4. For five min, cook.
5. Chop the spinach; add the cream cheese and 1 tsp of cream cheese. And black pepper.
6. Add 1/2 onion, cut into cubes, and then stir well.
7. Get the bowl out and beat the eggs well.

8. Shift the filling of the spinach into your crust and sprinkle it with cheese. Over it, pour your eggs, and then cook for seven min at 175 degs C.
9. Decrease the heat of your air fryer to 150 degs C, then cook for another 9 min. Before slicing to serve, allow it to cool.

Nutrition: Calories 154; Fat 1 g; Carbohydrates 13 g; Sugar 8 g; Protein 11 g;

Zucchini Gratin

Prep T: 10 min | Cook T: 12 min | Servings: 4

Ingredients

- Two Zucchini
- 1 Tablespoon Flour of Coconut
- 1 Parsley tbsp
- 1 Butter Teaspoon
- 140 grams of Cheese Parmesan, Shredded

Directions

1. In a tub, blend the coconut flour, black pepper and cheese together.
2. Shake well then cut your zucchini into slices. Cut the squares of your zucchini, and then spread them out in the air-fryer. Heat your air fryer to 205 degs C, then mix it all together and cook for 13 min.

Nutrition: Calories 154; Fat 1 g; Carbohydrates 13 g; Sugar 0 g; Protein 11 g; Cholesterol 0 mg;

Golden Eggplant Slices with Parsley

Prep T: 5 min | Cook T: 12 min | Servings: 4

Ingredients

- 128 grams flour
- 4 eggs
- Salt, to taste
- 256 grams bread crumbs
- 1 tsp Italian seasoning
- 2 eggplants, sliced
- 2 garlic cloves, sliced
- 2 tbsp chopped parsley
- Cooking Spray

Directions

1. Spritz the air fry basket with cooking spray. Set aside.
2. On a plate, place the flour. In a shallow bowl, whisk the eggs with salt. In another shallow bowl, combine the bread crumbs and Italian seasoning.

3. Dredge the eggplant slices, one at a time, in the flour, then in the whisked eggs, finally in the bread crumb mixture to coat well.
4. Lay the coated eggplant slices in the air fry basket.
5. Place the basket on the air fry position.
6. Select Air Fry, set temperature to 199 degs C, and set time to 12 min. Flip the eggplant slices halfway through the cooking time.
7. When cooking is complete, the eggplant slices should be golden brown and crispy. Transfer the eggplant slices to a plate and sprinkle the parsley and garlic on top before serving.

Nutrition: Calories 463; Fat 9.5 g; Carbohydrates 121 g; Protein 22 g; Fiber 12 g; Sugar 11.5 g;

Cheesy Potato Taquitos

Prep T: 5 min | Cook T: 6 min per batch | Makes 12 taquitos

Ingredients

- 256 grams mashed potatoes
- 64 grams shredded Mexican cheese
- 12 corn tortillas
- Cooking Spray

Directions

1. Line the baking pan with parchment paper.
2. Place the baking pan on the air fry position. Select Air Fry, set temperature to 204 degs C, and set the time to 6 min.
3. In a bowl, combine the potatoes and cheese until well mixed. Microwave the tortillas on high heat for 30 seconds or until softened. Add some water to another bowl and set alongside.
4. On a clean work surface lay the tortillas–scoop 3 tbsp of the panato mixture in each tortilla center. Roll up tightly and secure with toothpicks if necessary.
5. Arrange the filled tortillas, seam side down, in the prepared baking pan. Spritz the tortillas with cooking spray.
6. Air fry for 6 min, or until crispy and golden brown, flipping once halfway through the cooking time. You may need to work in batches to avoid overcrowding.
7. Serve hot.

Nutrition: Calories 160; Fat 3 g; Carbohydrates 25 g; Protein 5 g; Fiber 4 g; Sugar 0.5 g;

Broccoli Casserole

Prep T: 15 min | Cook T: 14 min | Servings: 4

Ingredients

- 512 grams steamed broccoli florets (about 1 large head), chopped
- 32 grams peeled diced yellow onion

- 64 grams diced white mushrooms
- 1 large egg
- 2 tbsp sour cream
- 32 grams mayonnaise
- 1 tsp salt
- 1/2 tsp freshly ground black pepper
- 128 grams coarsely crushed Cheddar cheese crisps

Directions

1. In a large bowl, combine broccoli, onion, mushrooms, egg, sour cream, mayonnaise, salt, and pepper. Spoon mixture into a round cake barrel.
2. Preheat air fryer at 177 degs C for 3 min.
3. Cook casserole 14 min.
4. Remove barrel from air fryer and let rest 10 min. Evenly distribute crushed Cheddar Cheese crisps over the top of casserole and serve warm.

Nutrition: Calories: 251; Protein: 10g; Fiber: 3g; Net Carbohydrates: 6g; Fat: 21g; Sodium: 896mg; Carbohydrates: 8g; Sugar: 2g;

Black Bean and Tomato Chili

Prep T: 15 min | Cook T: 23 min | Servings: 6

Ingredients

- 1 tbsp olive oil
- 1 medium onion, diced
- 3 garlic cloves, minced
- 128 grams vegetable broth
- 3 cans black beans, drained and rinsed
- 2 cans diced tomatoes
- 2 chipanle peppers, chopped
- 2 tsps cumin
- 2 tsps chili powder
- 1 tsp dried oregano
- 1/2 tsp salt

Directions

1. Over a medium heat, fry the garlic and onions in the olive oil for 3 min.
2. Add the remaining ingredients, stirring constantly and scraping the bottom to prevent sticking.
3. Place the baking pan on the bake position. Select Bake, set the temperature to 204 degs C, and set the time to 20 min.
4. Take the baking pan and place the mixture inside. Put a sheet of aluminum foil on top.
5. Bake for 20 min.
6. When ready, plate up and serve immediately.

Nutrition: Calories 372; Fat 3.5 g; Carbohydrates 65 g; Protein 22 g; Fiber 16 g; Sugar 5 g;

Cheesy Cauliflower Fritters

Prep T: 31 min | Cook T: 5 min | Servings: 8
Ingredients

- 64 grams chopped parsley
- 128 grams Italian breadcrumbs
- 42 grams shredded mozzarella cheese
- 42 grams shredded sharp cheddar cheese
- 1 egg
- 2 minced garlic cloves
- 3 chopped scallions
- 1 head of cauliflower

Directions

1. Rinse cauliflower and Place into a food processor and pulse 20-30 seconds till it looks like rice.
2. Attach cauliflower rice in a bowl and mix with pepper, salt, egg, cheeses, breadcrumbs, garlic, and scallions.
3. Make 15 patties of the mixture. Add more breadcrumbs if needed.
4. Heat the fryer with olive oil.
5. Cook 14 min at 200 degs C, flipping after 7 min.

Nutrition: Calories 254; Fat 15.2 g; Carbohydrates 11.9 g; Sugar 1 g; Protein 17.5 g; Cholesterol 0 mg;

Spinach Samosa

Prep T: 25 minutes | Cook T: 20 minutes | Servings: 6
Ingredients

- 1 tsp garlic, diced
- ¼ tsp ground ginger
- 1 tsp olive oil
- 1 tsp ground turmeric
- ½ tsp garam masala
- ½ tsp ground coriander
- ½ tsp chili flakes
- 128 grams spinach, chopped
- 3 spring onions, chopped
- 1 tsp tomato sauce
- 128 grams Mozzarella, shredded
- 64 grams almond flour
- ½ tsp baking powder
- Cooking Spray

Directions

1. Preheat the olive oil in the skillet. Add garlic and ground ginger. Cook the ingredients for 2 minutes over the medium heat. Stir them well. Then add 1 tsp of ground turmeric, garam masala, ground coriander, and chili flakes. Add spinach and stir the mixture well. Add spring onions and tomato sauce.
2. Stir the mixture well and cook it with the closed lid for 10 minutes over the low heat. The cooked spinach mixture should be very soft. Cool the spinach mixture. Meanwhile, make the samosa dough: microwave the cheese until it is melted. Then mix it up with almond flour and baking powder.
3. Knead the soft dough and put it on the baking paper. Cover the dough with the second baking paper and roll-up. Then cut the flat dough on the triangles.
4. Place the spinach mixture on every triangle and fold them in the shape of the samosa. Secure the edges of samosa well.

Preheat the air fryer to 190 degs C. Grease the basket of the air fryer with cooking spray.

5. Put the samosa in the air fryer in one layer and cook for 5 minutes. Then flip samosa on another side and cook it for 5 minutes or until the meal is light brown.

Nutrition: Calories: 42; Fat: 2.8g; Fiber: 0.7g; Carbs: 2.6g; Protein:2.2g

Stuffed Peppers

Prep T: 10 min | Cook T: 25 min | Servings: 6

Ingredients

*   3 bell peppers cut in half & remove seeds
*   32 grams feta cheese, crumbled
*   64 grams grape tomatoes, sliced
*   42 grams chickpeas, rinsed
*   1/2 tsp. oregano
*   2 garlic cloves, minced
*   192 grams cooked quinoa
*   1/2 tsp. salt

Directions

1. In a bowl, mix cooked quinoa, tomatoes, chickpeas, oregano, garlic, and salt.
2. Stuff quinoa mixture into the bell pepper halves and place in a baking dish.
3. Select bake mode. Place the temperature to 205 degs C and the timer for 25 min. Press start.
4. Let the air fryer preheat then insert the pizza rack into shelf position 5.
5. Place baking dish on the pizza rack and cook.
6. Top peppers with crumbled cheese and serve.

Nutrition: Calories 237; Fat 4.8 g; Carbohydrates 39.8 g; Sugar 4.9 g; Protein 2.6 g; Cholesterol 6 mg;

Yellow Squash-Carrots and Zucchini

Prep T: 5 min | Cook T: 30 min | Servings: 4

Ingredients

*   Carrots (226 grams)
*   Olive oil (6 tsp. - divided)
*   Lime (1 sliced into wedges)
*   Zucchini (453 grams sliced into 19 mm semi-circles)
*   Yellow squash (453 grams)
*   Tarragon leaves (1 tbsp.)
*   White pepper (0.5 tsp.)

*   Sea salt (1 tsp.)

Directions

1. Set the Air Fryer at 205 degs C.
2. Trim the stem and roots from the squash and zucchini.
3. Dice and add the carrots into a bowl with two tsps of oil.
4. Toss the carrots into the fryer basket. Prepare for 5 min.
5. Mix in the zucchini, oil, salt, and pepper in the bowl.
6. When the carrots are done, fold in the mixture. Cook 30 min.
7. Stir the mixture occasionally. Chop the tarragon and garnish using and lime wedges.

Nutrition: Protein: 7.4 g; Carbohydrates: 8.6 g; Fat: 9.4 g; Calories: 256;

Air-Fried Green Beans

Prep T: 10 min | Cook T: 10 min |Serving: 4

Ingredients

*   680 grams of French green beans, stems removed and blanched
*   ½ tbsp salt
*   227 grams of shallots, peeled and cut into quarters
*   1/2 tsp ground white pepper
*   ½ tbsp olive oil

Directions

1. Coat the vegetables with the rest of the ingredients in a bowl.
2. Transfer to the air fryer basket and air fry at 204 degs C for 10 min, making sure the green beans achieve a light brown color.
3. Serve hot.

Nutrition: Calories 106; Total Fat 2 g; Total Carbs21 g; Fiber 6.3 g; Sugar 12.5 g; Protein 9.8 g;

Grilled Cheese and Greens Sandwiches

Prep T: 5 min | Cook T: 8 min | Servings: 4

Ingredients

*   192 gramss chopped mixed greens
*   2 garlic cloves, thinly sliced
*   2 tsps olive oil
*   2 slices low-sodium low-fat Swiss cheese
*   4 slices low-sodium whole-wheat bread
*   Olive oil spray, for coating the sandwiches

Directions

1. In a 15-by-5-cm pan, mix the greens, garlic, and olive oil. Grill in the air fryer for 4 to 5 min, stirring once, until the vegetables are tender. Drain, if necessary.
2. Make 2 sandwiches, dividing half of the greens and 1 slice of Swiss cheese between 2 slices of bread. Lightly spray the outsides of the sandwiches with olive oil spray.
3. Grill the sandwiches in the air fryer for 6 to 8 min. Cut each sandwich in half to serve.

Nutrition: Calories 176; Fat 6 g; Carbohydrates 24 g; Sugar 0 g; Protein 10 g; Cholesterol 0 mg;

Fast Roasted Maitake Mushrooms

Prep T: 5 min | Cook T: 15 min |Serving: 2

Ingredients

- 1 tbsp soy sauce
- 1 tsps toasted sesame oil
- 1 tsps vegetable oil, divided
- 1 garlic clove, minced
- 198 grams of maitake (hen of the woods) mushrooms
- 1/2 tsp flaky sea salt
- 1/2 tsp sesame seeds
- 1/2 tsp finely chopped fresh thyme leaves

Directions

1. Whisk together the soy sauce, sesame oil, 1 tsp of vegetable oil, and garlic in a small bowl.
2. Arrange the mushrooms in the air fryer basket in a single layer. Drizzle the soy sauce mixture over the mushrooms. Roast at 149 degs C for 10 min.
3. Flip the mushrooms and sprinkle the sea salt, sesame seeds, and thyme leaves on top. Drizzle the remaining 2 tsps of vegetable oil all over. Roast for an additional 5 min.
4. Remove the mushrooms from the basket to a plate and serve hot.

Nutrition: Calories: 70; Fat: 2.5 g; Protein: 1.5g; Carbs: 6.5 g; Sugar: 2 g;

Golden Cheesy Corn Casserole

Prep T: 5 min | Cook T: 15 min | Servings: 4

Ingredients

- 256 grams frozen yellow corn
- 1 egg, beaten
- 3 tbsp flour
- 64 grams grated Swiss or Havarti cheese
- 64 grams light cream
- 32 ml milk
- Pinch salt
- Freshly ground black pepper, to taste
- 2 tbsp butter, cut into cubes
- Nonstick cooking spray

Directions

1. Spritz a baking pan with nonstick cooking spray.
2. Stir together the remaining ingredients except for the butter in a medium bowl until well incorporated. Transfer the mixture to the prepared baking pan and scatter with the butter cubes.
3. Place the pan on the bake position.
4. Select Bake, set temperature to 160 degs C, and set time to 15 min.
5. When cooking is complete, the top should be golden brown, and a toothpick inserted in the center should come out clean. Remove the pan from the air fryer grill.

6. Let the casserole cool for 5 min before slicing into wedges and serving.

Nutrition: Calories 220; Fat 12.8 g; Carbohydrates 17.5 g; Protein 9.3 g; Fiber 1.8 g; Sugar 4.5 g;

Corn and Bell Pepper Casserole

Prep T: 10 min | Cook T: 20 min | Servings: 4

Ingredients:

- 128 grams corn kernels
- 32 grams bell pepper, finely chopped
- 64 ml low-fat milk
- 1 large egg, beaten
- 64 grams yellow cornmeal
- 64 grams all-purpose flour
- 1/2 tsp baking powder
- 2 tbsp melted unsalted butter
- 1 tbsp granulated sugar
- Pinch of cayenne pepper
- 1/4 tsp kosher salt
- Cooking Spray

Directions:

1. Spritz a baking pan with cooking spray.
2. Combine all your ingredients in a very large bowl. Stir to mix well. Pour the mixture into the baking pan.
3. Place the pan on the bake position.
4. Select Bake, set temperature to 166 degs C and set time to 20 min.
5. When cooking is complete, the casserole should be lightly browned and set.
6. Remove the baking pan from the air fryer grill and serve immediately.

Nutrition: Calories: 249; Fat: 8 g; Protein: 5.5 g; Carbs: 38.5 g; Net Carbs: 6.5 g; Fiber: 2.8 g; Sugar: 4 g

Curried Tofu and Turmeric Cauli Rice

Prep T: 5 min | Cook T: 16 min | Servings: 4

Ingredients

- 226 grams of extra-firm tofu, pressed and cut into 0.6 cm cubes
- 64 ml canned unsweetened coconut milk
- 2 tsps red curry paste
- 2 cloves garlic, peeled and minced
- 1 tbsp avocado oil
- 1 tbsp coconut oil
- 1 small head cauliflower, pulsed into rice

- 1 tbsp turmeric powder
- 1/2 tsp salt
- 1/2 tsp freshly ground white pepper
- 4 lime wedges
- 32 grams chopped fresh cilantro

Directions

1. In a medium bowl, combine tofu, coconut milk, red curry paste, garlic, and avocado oil. Refrigerate covered 30 min.
2. Preheat air fryer at 176 degs C for 3 min.
3. Place tofu and marinade in an ungreased cake barrel. Place in air fryer basket and cook 5 min. Stir, and then cook an additional 5 min.
4. While tofu is cooking, heat coconut oil in a medium skillet over medium-high heat for 30 seconds. Add rice cauliflower, turmeric powder, salt, and pepper. Stir-fry 6 min until cauliflower is tender to your preference.
5. Add cauliflower to four medium bowls. Top with tofu mixture and sauce. Garnish with lime wedges and cilantro. Serve warm.

Nutrition: Calories: 177; Protein: 9g; Fiber: 4g; Net Carbohydrates: 7g; Fat: 12g; Sodium: 532mg; Carbohydrates: 12g; Sugar: 3g;

Chicken Drumsticks with Barbecue Sauce

Prep T: 5 min | Cook T: 18 min | Servings: 5

Ingredients

- 1 tbsp olive oil
- 10 chicken drumsticks
- Chicken seasoning or rub, to taste
- Salt and ground black pepper, to taste
- 128 grams barbecue sauce
- 32 grams honey

Directions

1. Grease the air fry basket with olive oil.
2. Season the chicken thighs with chicken seasoning or rub, salt and pepper.
3. Arrange the chicken drumsticks in the air fry basket.
4. Place the basket on the air fry position.
5. Select Air Fry. Set temperature to 199 degs C and set time to 18 min. Flip the drumsticks halfway through.
6. When cooking is complete, the drumsticks should be lightly browned.
7. Meanwhile, combine the honey and barbecue sauce in a small bowl. Stir to mix well.
8. Remove the drumsticks from the air fryer grill and baste with the sauce mixture to serve.

Nutrition: Calories 338; Fat 28 g; Carbohydrates 11.5 g; Protein 9 g; Fiber 0.2 g; Sugar 9.5 g;

Italian Cheese Marinara Chicken Breasts

Prep T: 30 min | Cook T: 1 hour | Servings: 2

Ingredients

- 1 large egg
- 32 grams almond meal
- 340 grams of boneless, skinless chicken breast halves
- 227 grams of jar marinara sauce, divided
- 4 tbsp shredded Mozzarella cheese, divided
- 4 tbsp grated Parmesan cheese, divided
- 4 tbsp chopped fresh basil, divided
- Salt and freshly ground black pepper, to taste
- Cooking Spray

Directions

1. Spritz the air fry basket with cooking spray.
2. In a shallow bowl, beat the egg.
3. In a separate shallow bowl, place the almond meal.
4. Dip 1 chicken breast half into the egg, then into the almond meal to coat. Place the coated chicken in the air fry basket. Repeat with the remaining 1 chicken breast half.
5. Place the basket on the bake position.
6. Select Bake, set temperature to 180 degs C and set time to 40 min.
7. After 20 min, remove the basket from the air fryer grill and flip the chicken. Return the basket to the air fryer grill and continue cooking.
8. When cooking is complete, the chicken should no longer pink and the juices run clear.
9. In a baking pan, pour half of marinara sauce.
10. Place the cooked chicken in the sauce. Cover with the remaining marinara.
11. Sprinkle 2 tbsp of Mozzarella cheese and 2 tbsp of soy Parmesan cheese on each chicken breast. Top each with 2 tbsp of basil.
12. Place the baking pan back in the air fryer grill and set the baking time to 20 min. Flip the chicken halfway through the cooking time.
13. When cooking is complete, an instant-read thermometer inserted into the center of the chicken should read at least 74 degs C.
14. Remove the pan from the air fryer grill and divide between 2 plates. Season with salt and pepper and serve.

Nutrition: Calories 469; Fat 21 g; Carbohydrates 8 g; Protein 58 g; Fiber 1.5 g; Sugar 5 g;

Air Fryer Chicken Nuggets

Prep/Cook Time: 22 min | Servings: 4

Ingredients

- 1/4 cup whole wheat flour
- 1/4 tsp salt, or to taste
- 1/4 teaspoon black pepper
- 1 large egg
- 2/3 cup whole wheat panko bread crumbs
- 1/3 cup grated Parmesan cheese
- 2 teaspoons dried parsley flakes
- 453 grams of boneless, skinless chicken breasts, cut into 2,5 cm cubes
- Olive oil spray

Optional dipping sauce:

- marinara or pizza sauce, barbecue sauce, or ranch dressing

Directions

1. Preheat air fryer at 205 degs C for 8-10 min.
2. Set out three small shallow bowls. In the first bowl, place flour, salt, and pepper; mix lightly. In the second bowl, add egg and beat lightly.
3. In the third bowl, combine Panko, parmesan cheese,and parsley flakes.
4. One at a time, coat chicken pieces in the flour mixture, then dip into the beaten egg, and finally coat with the Panko mixture, pressing lightly to help the coating
5. adhere.
6. Place chicken nuggets in basket of air fryer, in a single layer. Spray the nuggets with olive oil spray (this helps them get golden brown and crispy). You will not
7. be able to cook them all at once. Cook each batch of chicken nuggets for 7 min, or until internal temperature reaches 74 degs C. Do not overcook.

Nutrition: Calories 256; Fat 5.5 g; Carbohydrates 16 g; Protein 33 g; Fiber 1.2 g; Sugar 1 g;

Spiced Breaded Chicken Cutlets

Prep T: 5 min | Cook T: 11 min | Servings: 2

Ingredients

- 227 grams of boneless, skinless chicken breasts, horizontally sliced in half, into cutlets
- 1/2 tbsp extra-virgin olive oil
- 16 grams bread crumbs
- 1/4 tsp sea salt
- 1/4 tsp freshly ground black pepper
- 1/4 tsp paprika
- 1/4 tsp garlic powder
- 1/8 tsp onion powder

Directions

1. Place the crisper tray on the air fry position. Select Air Fry, temperature to 191 degs C, and set the time to 11 min.
2. Brush each side with the oil.
3. Combine the bread crumbs, salt, pepper, paprika, garlic powder, and onion powder in a medium shallow bowl. Dredge the chicken cutlets in the bread crumb mixture, turning several times, to ensure the chicken is fully coated.
4. Place the chicken in the crisper tray. Air fry for 9 min. Cooking is done when the internal temperature reaches at least 74 degs C on a food thermometer. If needed Air fry for up to 2 min more.
5. Remove the chicken cutlets and serve immediately.

Nutrition: Calories 216; Fat 7 g; Carbohydrates 7.5 g; Protein 29 g; Fiber 0 g; Sugar 0.5 g;

Pesto Chicken

Prep T: 10 min | Cook T: 20 min |Serve: 2

Ingredients

- 4 chicken drumsticks
- 6 garlic cloves
- 1/2 jalapeno pepper
- 2 tbsp. lemon juice
- 2 tbsp. olive oil
- 1 tbsp. ginger, sliced
- 64 grams cilantro
- 1 tsp. salt

Directions

1. Add all the ingredients except chicken into the blender and blend until smooth.
2. Pour blended mixture into the large bowl.
3. Add chicken and stir well to coat. Place in refrigerator for 2 hours.
4. Spray air fryer basket with cooking spray.
5. Place marinated chicken into the air fryer basket and cook at 200 degs C for 20 min. Turn halfway through.

6. Serve and enjoy.

Nutrition: Calories 305; Fat 19 g; Carbohydrates 5 g; Sugar 0.7 g; Protein 25 g; Cholesterol 80 mg;

Turkey Meatballs

Prep T: 10 min | Cook T: 12 min | Servings: 4

Ingredients

- 453 grams of ground turkey
- 2 garlic cloves, minced
- 32 grams carrots, grated
- 1 egg, lightly beaten
- 2 tbsp. coconut flour
- 2 green onion, chopped
- 32 grams celery, chopped
- Pepper
- Salt

Directions

1. Spray air fryer basket with cooking spray.
2. Preheat the air fryer to 205 degs C.
3. Get a bowl and add all the ingredients by mixing them together.
4. Make balls from meat mixture and place into the air fryer basket and cook for 12 min. Turn halfway through.
5. Serve and enjoy.

Nutrition: Calories 275; Fat 13 g; Carbohydrates 6 g; Sugar 1 g; Protein 34 g; Cholesterol 125 mg;

Chicken Couscous Bowl

Prep T: 10 min | Cook T: 25 min | Servings: 2

Ingredients

- Water 120 ml
- Tomato purees 2 tbsp.
- Vegetable stock cube 1/2
- Couscous 120 grams
- Sriracha sauce 1 tbsp.
- Chicken breasts, sliced 2
- Oil 1 tbsp.
- Tomatoes 2, diced
- Paprika 1 tsp.
- Garlic powder 1 tsp.
- Onion 1, peeled and diced
- Salt and pepper
- Bell pepper 1, deseeded and diced
- For garnishing parsley feta and cheese

Directions

1. Boil 120 ml of water and transfer some of the vegetable stock. Stir until the stock dissolves. In a bowl put the couscous and pour over it with vegetable stock. Cover and set the bowl on the side.
2. Ensure that a pot is placed, but remove the grill plate. Choose ROAST, set the temp to 200 degs C, and set the timer for 15 min. To commence preheating, click START/STOP.
3. Mix the chicken, paprika, oil, garlic powder, pepper, and salt together in a dish.
4. Once the device beeps to signal that it has preheated, insert the seasoned chicken and close the lid to start cooking.
5. Open the cover and put bell pepper, tomatoes and onion when 10 min are remaining on the timer. To keep cooking, close the lid.

6. Insert Sriracha, tomato puree and already cooked couscous and mix well when there are 3 min left on the timer.
7. Stir in the parsley and garnish with the feta cheese until the cooking phase has been finished. Serve it hot.

Nutrition: Calories: 271; Proteins 29g; Carbs: 20g; Fat: 15g

Maple-Teriyaki Chicken Wings

Prep T: 5 min | Cook T: 14 min | Servings: 4

Ingredients

- 128 grams maple syrup
- 42 grams soy sauce
- 32 grams teriyaki sauce
- 3 garlic cloves, minced
- 2 tsps garlic powder
- 2 tsps onion powder
- 1 tsp freshly ground black pepper
- 907 grams of bone-in chicken wings (drumettes and flats)

Directions

1. Place the grill plate on the grill position. Select Grill, set the temperature to 177 degs C, and set the time to 14 min.
2. Meanwhile, in a large bowl, whisk the maple syrup, soy sauce, teriyaki sauce, garlic, garlic powder, onion powder, and black pepper. Add the wings, and use tongs to toss and coat.
3. Place the chicken wings on the grill plate. Grill for 5 min. After 5 min, flip the wings and grill for an additional 5 min.
4. Check the wings for doneness. Cooking is done when the internal temperature reaches at minimum 74 degs C on a food thermometer. If needed, grill for up to 4 min more.
5. Remove from the grill and serve.

Nutrition: Calories 559; Fat 29 g; Carbohydrates 41.5 g; Protein 39.3 g; Fiber 0 g; Sugar 37.5 g;

Chicken Tenders

Prep T: 10 min | Cook T: 12 min | Servings: 4

Ingredients

- 453 grams of chicken tenders
- 1 egg, lightly beaten
- 96 grams pecans, crushed
- 32 grams ground mustard
- 1/2 tsp. paprika
- 1/4 tsp. garlic powder
- 1/4 tsp. onion powder
- 1/4 tsp. pepper
- 1 tsp. salt

Directions

1. Spray air fryer basket with cooking spray.
2. Add chicken into the large bowl. Season with paprika, pepper, garlic powder, onion powder, and salt. Add mustard mix well.
3. In a separate bowl, add egg and whisk well.
4. In a shallow bowl, add crushed pecans.
5. Dip chicken into the egg then coats with pecans and place into the air fryer basket.
6. Cook at 177 degs C for 12 min.
7. Serve and enjoy.

Nutrition: Calories 481; Fat 31 g; Carbohydrates 7 g; Sugar 2 g; Protein 40 g; Cholesterol 145 mg;

Classic Turkey Schnitzel

Prep T: 10 min | Cook T: 15 min | Servings: 3

Ingredients

- 680 grams of turkey thighs, skinless, boneless
- 1 egg, beaten
- 64 grams all-purpose flour
- 64 grams seasoned breadcrumbs
- 1/2 tsp red pepper flakes, crushed
- Sea salt and ground black pepper, to taste
- 1 tbsp olive oil

Directions

1. Flatten the turkey thighs with a mallet.
2. Whisk the egg in a shallow bowl. Place the flour in a second bowl.
3. Then, in a third shallow bowl, place the breadcrumbs, red pepper, salt, and black pepper. Soak the turkey first in the flour, then, in the beaten egg, and roll them in the breadcrumb mixture.
4. Place the breaded turkey thighs in the Air Fryer basket. Mist your schnitzel with the olive oil and transfer them to the cooking basket.
5. Cook the schnitzel at 194 degs C for 22 min, turning them over halfway through the cooking time.

Nutrition: Calories: 279; Fat: 18 g; Carbs: 8 g; Sugar: 1.5 g; Protein:20 g; Cholesterol: 0 mg

Pomegranate Chicken Breasts with Salad

Prep T: 25 min | Cook T: 20 min | Servings: 4

Ingredients

- 3 tbsp plus 2 tsps pomegranate molasses
- 1⁄2 tsp ground cinnamon
- 1 tsp minced fresh thyme
- Salt and ground black pepper, to taste
- 680 grams of bone-in split chicken breasts, trimmed
- 32 ml chicken broth
- 32 grams water
- 64 grams couscous
- 1 tbsp minced fresh parsley
- 57 grams of cherry tomatoes, quartered
- 1 scallion, white part minced, green part sliced thin on bias
- 1 tbsp extra-virgin olive oil
- 28 grams of feta cheese, crumbled
- Cooking Spray

Directions

1. Spritz the air fry basket with cooking spray.
2. Combine 3 tbsp of pomegranate molasses, thyme, cinnamon, and 1⁄8 tsp of salt in a small bowl. Stir to mix well. Set aside.
3. Place the chicken breasts in the air fry basket, skin side down, and spritz with cooking spray. Sprinkle with salt and ground black pepper.
4. Place the basket on the air fry position.
5. Select Air Fry. Set temperature to 180 degs C and set time to 20 min. Flip the chicken and brush with pomegranate molasses mixture halfway through.
6. Meanwhile, pour the broth and water in a pot and bring to a boil over medium-high heat. Add the couscous and sprinkle with salt. Cover and simmer for 7 min or until the liquid is almost absorbed.
7. Combine the remaining ingredients, except for the cheese, with cooked couscous in a large bowl. Toss to mix well. Scatter with the feta cheese.
8. Once cooking is done, remove the chicken from the air fryer grill and allow to cool for 10 min. Serve with vegetable and couscous salad.

*Nutrition: Calories **266**; Fat **7.5** g; Carbohydrates **19** g; Protein **28.3** g; Fiber **1.5** g; Sugar **1.3** g;*

Chicken and Asparagus

Prep T: 5 minutes | Cook T: 20 minutes | Servings: 4

Ingredients

- 4 chicken breasts, skinless, boneless and halved
- 1 tbsp sweet paprika
- bunch asparagus, trimmed and halved
- 1 tbsp olive oil
- Salt and black pepper to the taste

Directions

1. Get a bowl and mix all the ingredients in it,put them in your Air Fryer's basket and cook at 200 degs C for 20 minutes.
2. Divide between plates and serve for lunch.

Nutrition: Calories: 230; Fat: 11g; Fiber: 3g; Carbs: 5g; Protein:12g

Buttermilk Marinated Chicken Wings

Prep T: 1 hour 20 min | Cook T: 17 to 19 min | Servings: 4

Ingredients:

- 907 grams of chicken wings

Marinade:

- 128 grams buttermilk
- 1⁄2 tsp salt
- 1⁄2 tsp black pepper

Coating:

- 128 grams flour
- 128 grams panko bread crumbs
- 2 tbsp poultry seasoning
- 2 tsps salt
- Cooking Spray

Directions:

1. Get a bowl and mix together all the ingredients for the marinade.
2. Dip the chicken wings in the bowl with the marinade and let them rest in the refrigerator for at least an hour (the more they marinate, the tastier they will be).
3. Spritz the crisper tray with cooking spray.
4. Place the crisper tray on the air fry position. Select Air Fry, set the temperature to 182 degs C, and set the time to 19 min.
5. Get a deep bowl and add all the ingredients for the coating by giving it a stir.
6. Remove the chicken wings from the bowl and let the excess marinade drip off.
   Once done bread them in the coating mixture.
7. Place the chicken wings in the crisper tray in a single layer. Mist the wings with cooking spray. You'll need to work in batches to avoid overcrowding.
8. Air fry for 17 to 19 min, or until the wings are crisp and golden brown on the outside. Flip the wings halfway through the cooking time.
9. Remove from the crisper tray to a plate and repeat with the remaining wings.
10. Serve hot.

Nutrition: Calories 773; Fat 34 g; Carbohydrates 53 g; Protein 60 g; Fiber 4 g; Sugar 16 g;

Turkey with Tabasco Sauce

Prep T: 15 min | Cook T: 22 min | Servings: 6
Ingredients

- 680 grams of ground turkey
- 6 whole eggs, well beaten
- 1/3 tsp smoked paprika
- 2 egg whites, beaten

- Tabasco sauce, for drizzling
- 2 tbsp sesame oil
- 2 leeks, chopped
- 3 cloves garlic, finely minced
- 1⁄2 tsp ground black pepper
- 1⁄2 tsp sea salt

Directions

1. Warmth the oil in a pan over moderate heat; then, sweat the leeks and garlic until tender; stir periodically.
2. Next, grease 6 oven safe ramekins with pan spray. Divide the sautéed mixture among six ramekins.
3. In a bowl, beat the eggs and egg whites using a wire whisk. Stir in the smoked paprika, salt and black pepper; whisk until everything is thoroughly combined. Divide the egg mixture among the ramekins.
4. Air-fry approximately 22 min at 174 degs C. Drizzle Tabasco sauce over each portion and serve.

Nutrition: Calories: 298; Fat: 15g; Protein:6g; Carbs: 25g; Net Carbs: 24g; Fiber: 1g

Turkey and Avocado Sliders

Prep T: 15 min | Cook T: 25 min | Servings: 4
Ingredients

- 450 grams of turkey, ground
- 1 tbsp olive oil
- 1 avocado, peeled, pitted and chopped
- 1 garlic cloves, minced
- 64 grams breadcrumbs
- Kosher salt and ground pepper, to taste
- 8 small rolls

Directions

1. Mix the turkey, olive oil, avocado, garlic, breadcrumbs, salt, and black pepper until everything is well combined. Form the mixture into eight small patties.
2. Cook the patties at 194 degs C for about 20 min or until cooked through; make sure to turn them over halfway through the cooking time.
3. Serve your patties in the prepared rolls and enjoy!

Nutrition: Calories: 250; Protein: 30 g; Fiber: 1.5 g; Fat: 10 g; Carbohydrates: 10 g; Sugar: 1.25 g;

Parsley Turkey Stew

Prep T: 5 minutes | Cook T: 25 minutes | Servings: 4
Ingredients

- 1 turkey breast, skinless, boneless and cubed
- 1 tbsp olive oil
- 1 broccoli head, florets separated
- 128 grams keto tomato sauce
- Salt and black pepper to the taste
- 1 tbsp parsley, chopped

Directions

1. In a baking dish that fits your air fryer, mix the turkey with the rest of the ingredients except the parsley, toss, introduce the dish in the fryer, bake at 193 degs C for 25 minutes, divide into bowls, sprinkle the parsley on top and serve.

Nutrition: Calories: 250; Fat: 11g; Fiber: 2g; Carbs: 6g; Protein:12g

Chicken Tenders with Mushroom Sauce

Prep T: 25 min | Cook T: 30 min | Servings: 4

Ingredients

- 1 tbsp melted butter
- 32 grams all-purpose flour
- 4 chicken tenders, cut in half crosswise
- 4 slices ham, 6 mm thick, large enough to cover an English muffin
- 2 English muffins, split in halves
- Salt and ground black pepper, to taste
- Cooking Spray

Mushroom Sauce:

- 2 tbsp butter
- 64 grams chopped mushrooms
- 64 grams chopped green onions
- 2 tbsp flour
- 128 ml chicken broth
- 1.1⁄2 tsps Worcestershire sauce
- 1⁄4 tsp garlic powder

Directions

1. Put the butter in a baking pan. Combine the salt, flour, and ground black pepper in a shallow dish. Roll the chicken tenders over to coat well.
2. Arrange the chicken in the pan, flip to coat with the melted butter.
3. Place the pan on the broil position.
4. Select Broil, set temperature to 199 degs C and set time to 10 min. Flip the tenders halfway through.
5. When cooking is complete, the juices of chicken tenders should run clear.
6. Meanwhile, make the mushroom sauce: melt 2 tbsp of butter in a saucepan over medium-high heat.
7. Add the mushrooms and onions to the saucepan and sauté for 3 min or until the onions are translucent.
8. Gently mix in the flour, Worcestershire sauce, garlic powder, and broth until smooth.
9. Reduce the heat to low and simmer 5 min or until it has a thick consistency. Set the sauce aside until it is ready to serve.
10. When broiling is complete, remove the baking pan from the air fryer grill and set the ham slices into the air fry basket.
11. Select Air Fry. Set time to 5 min. Flip the ham slices halfway through.
12. When cooking is complete, the ham slices should be heated through.
13. Remove the ham slices from the air fryer grill and set in the English muffin halves and warm for 1 min.
14. Arrange each of them on top of each muffin half, then place each chicken tender over the ham slice.
15. Transfer to the air fryer grill and set time to 2 min on Air Fry.
16. Serve with the sauce on top.

Nutrition: Calories 300; Fat 11 g; Carbohydrates 28 g; Protein 22 g; Fiber 1.5 g; Sugar 0.5 g;

Curry Chicken with Sweet Potato

Prep T: 10 min | Cook T: 20 min | Servings: 4

Ingredients

- 454 grams of boneless, skinless chicken thighs
- 1 tsp kosher salt, divided
- 32 grams unsalted butter, melted
- 1 tbsp curry powder
- 2 medium sweet potatoes, peeled and cut in 2.5 cm cubes
- 340 grams of Brussels sprouts, halved

Directions

1. Sprinkle the chicken thighs with 1⁄2 tsp of kosher salt. Place them in the single layer on a baking pan.
2. In a small bowl, stir together the butter and curry powder.
3. Place the sweet potatoes and Brussels sprouts in a large bowl. Drizzle half the curry butter over the vegetables and add the remaining kosher salt. Toss to coat. Transfer the vegetables to the baking pan and place in a single layer around the chicken. Brush half of the remaining curry butter over the chicken.
4. Place the pan on the toast position.
5. Select Toast, set temperature to 205 degs C, and set time to 20 min.
6. After 10 min, remove the pan from the air fryer grill and turn over the chicken thighs. Baste them with the remaining curry butter. Return the pan to the air fryer grill and continue cooking.
7. Cooking is complete when the sweet potatoes are tender and the chicken is cooked through and reads 74 degs C on a meat thermometer.

Nutrition: Calories 364; Fat 19 g; Carbohydrates 23.5 g; Protein 24.3 g; Fiber 4.8 g; Sugar 7 g;

Korean Chicken Tenders

Prep T: 10 min | Cook T: 10 min | Servings: 3

Ingredients

- 340 grams of chicken tenders, skinless and boneless
- 2 tbsp. green onion, chopped
- 3 garlic cloves, chopped
- 2 tsp. sesame seeds, toasted
- 1 tbsp ginger, grated
- 32 grams sesame oil
- 64 grams soy sauce
- 1/4 tsp. pepper

Directions

1. Slide chicken tenders onto the skewers.
2. In a large bowl, mix together green onion, garlic, sesame seeds, ginger, sesame oil, soy sauce, and pepper.
3. Add chicken skewers into the bowl and coat well with marinade. Place in refrigerator for overnight.
4. Preheat the air fryer to 200 degs C.
5. Place marinated chicken skewers into the air fryer basket and cook for 10 min .

Nutrition: Calories 334; Fat 17 g; Carbohydrates 0.6 g; Sugar 1 g; Protein 32 g;

Buttered Duck Breasts

Prep T: 11 min | Cook T: 42 min | Servings: 2
Ingredients

- unsalted butter (3 tbsp)
- duck breasts (340 grams)
- Salt
- dried thyme (1/2 tsp)
- black pepper
- star anise powder (1/4 tsp)

Directions

1. Heat your Air fryer; grease your air fryer bucket.
2. Season the duck breasts with black pepper and salt.
3. Place the breasts into your air fryer bucket; cook for around 10 min.
4. Place the breasts in a dish and spatter with dissolved butter.
5. Season the breasts with star anise powder and thyme.
6. Put them again inside your Air fryer bucket.
7. Cook for approximately 12 more min.
8. Distribute instantly to serve warm.

Nutrition: Calories 296; Fat 15.5 g; Carbohydrates 0.1 g; Sugar 0 g; Protein 37.5 g; Cholesterol 0 mg;

Simple Turkey Breast

Prep T: 29 min | Cook T: 40 min | Servings: 10
Ingredients

- turkey breast (3.6 kg)
- olive oil
- black pepper and salt

Directions

1. Heat your Air fryer
2. Grease an Air fryer bucket.
3. Season the breast with black pepper and salt, sprinkle with oil.
4. Place the breast into your Air Fryer bucket, cook for approximately 20 min.
5. Flip the surface, cook for additional 20 min.
6. Distribute in a plate and slice into aspired size.

Nutrition: Calories 549; Fat 24.5 g; Carbohydrates 0 g; Sugar 0 g; Protein 76.5 g;

Turkey and Mushroom Stew

Prep T: 14 min | Cook T: 12 min | Servings: 6
Ingredients

- Brown mushrooms; sliced (226 grams)
- 1 turkey breast, boneless and browned
- black pepper, salt
- Parsley; minced (1 tbsp.)
- tomato sauce

Directions

1. Add mushrooms, pepper, turkey, tomato sauce and salt to your air fryer pan, mix well.
2. Arrange the pan in your air fryer.
3. Cook for around 15 min at 188 degs C.
4. Distribute among plates.
5. Sprinkle the parsley on the top, serve.

Nutrition: Calories 220; Fat 5 g; Carbohydrates 5 g; Sugar 0 g; Protein 12 g; Cholesterol 0 mg;

Ground Chicken Meatballs

Prep T: 8 min | Cook T: 32 min | Servings: 4
Ingredients

- garlic powder, salt
- Ground Chicken (453 grams)
- panko (42 grams)
- One egg
- chives (2 tsps)
- thyme (1 tsp)

Directions

1. Merge the ingredients to a shallow bowl; toss well.
2. Shape humble meatballs out this mix-up.
3. Put the meatballs in your air fryer bucket.
4. Switch the "Power Button" of your air fryer; pick the "Air Fry" mode.
5. Touch the Time code and set the cooking period to almost 10 min.
6. Now start the Temp switch to Set the temperature at 176 degs C.
7. When prepared, serve warm.

Nutrition: Calories 207; Fat 10.4 g; Carbohydrates 5 g; Protein 23.2 g; Fiber: 0.25 g; Sugar 0.5 g;

Fast Old Bay Chicken Wings

Prep T: 10 min | Cook T: 13 min | Servings: 4

Ingredients

- 2 tbsp Old Bay seasoning
- 2 tsps baking powder
- 2 tsps salt
- 907 grams of chicken wings , patted dry
- Cooking Spray

Directions

1. Combine the Old Bay seasoning, salt, and baking powder in a large zip-top plastic bag. Add the chicken wings, seal, and shake until the wings are thoroughly coated in the seasoning mixture.
2. Lightly spray the air fry basket with cooking spray. Lay the chicken wings in the air fry basket in a single layer and lightly mist them with cooking spray.
3. Place the basket on the air fry position.
4. Select Air Fry, set temperature to 205 degs C, and set time to 13 min. Flip the wings halfway through the cooking time.
5. When cooking is complete, the wings should reach an internal temperature of 74 degs C on a meat thermometer. Remove from the air fryer grill to a plate and serve hot.

Nutrition: Calories 324; Fat 8 g; Carbohydrates 0 g; Protein 63 g; Fiber 0 g;

Chapter 6: Red Meat

Carne Asada

Prep T: 5 min | Cook T: 15 min | Servings: 8

Ingredients

- 3 chipotle peppers in adobo, chopped
- 42 grams chopped fresh oregano
- 42 grams chopped fresh parsley
- 4 cloves garlic, minced
- Juice of 2 limes
- 1 tsp ground cumin seeds
- 42 grams olive oil
- 454 grams to 680 grams of flank steak
- Salt, to taste

Directions

1. Merge the chipotle, oregano, parsley, garlic, lime juice, cumin, and olive oil in a large bowl. Stir to mix well.
2. Dunk the flank steak in the mixture and press to coat well. Cover the bowl in plastic and marinate under room temperature for at least 30 min.
3. Detach the marinade and place the steak in the air fry basket. Sprinkle with salt.
4. Select Air Fry, Convection. Set temperature to 199 degs C and set time to 15 min. Press Start to begin preheating.
5. Once preheated, place the basket on the air fry position. Cook the steak halfway through the cooking time.
6. When cooking is processed, the steak should be medium-rare or reach your desired doneness.
7. Remove the steak from the oven and slice to serve.

Nutrition: Calories 350; Fat 13 g; Carbohydrates 1 g; Sugar 0 g; Protein 6 g; Cholesterol 0 mg;

Spareribs with Ketchup-Garlic Sauce

Prep T: 15 min | Cook T: 3 1/2 hours | Servings: 4 to 6

Ingredients

- 2 racks spareribs

Sauce:

- 1 tbsp olive oil
- 2 cloves garlic, minced
- 128 grams ketchup
- 96 ml water
- 42 grams packed brown sugar
- 1 tbsp paprika
- 2 tsps mild chili powder
- 1/4 tsp cayenne

Rub:

- 42 grams packed brown sugar
- 2 tbsp paprika
- 2 tsps salt
- 2 tsps soft chili powder
- 1 tsp onion powder
- 1/2 tsp garlic powder
- 1/4 tsp cayenne

Directions

1. For the sauce: Warm up the oil in a medium-size saucepan over medium heat and sauté the garlic for 15 seconds, until aromatic. Add remaining sauce ingredients and simmer for 5 min, stirring often. Remove from the heat and let cool before using.
2. For the rub: mix the rub ingredients in a tiny bowl, set aside.
3. Place ribs on a cutting board and pat dry with paper towels. Cut away any excess fat from the ribs. Remove the membrane from the ribs' back by using a blunt knife to work the membrane away from the bone in one corner. Grab hold of the membrane with paper towel for a good grip and gently peel away.
4. Lay the rib racks meat-side down. Apply a small portion of the rub, just enough to season, to the bone side of the racks. Lay one rack on top of the other, bone side to bone side, to form an even shape. Tie the two racks together with kitchen twine between every other bone. The ribs should be held tightly together. Run the rotisserie spit between the racks and secure it with the forks. The fork tines should run through the meat as best as possible. The ribs will move a little as the rotisserie turns. They should not flop around, however. Secure to prevent this. Apply the remaining rub evenly over the outer surface of the ribs. A general rule with rubs is that what sticks is the amount needed.
5. Select Grill, set the temperature to 190 degs C and set the time to 3 1/2 hours.
6. Place the ribs in the grill and set a drip tray underneath. Roast until the ribs reach an internal temperature of 185 degs C. Test the temperature in several locations. Baste the ribs several times with the sauce during the last hour of cooking to build up a sticky surface.
7. Remove from the heat, carefully remove the rotisserie forks, slide the spit out, and then set the ribs on a large cutting board. Tent with foil and let the meat rest for 5 to 10 min. Cut away the twine and cut the racks into individual ribs.
8. Serve.

Nutrition for 4: Calories 451; Fat 35 g; Carbohydrates 5 g; Protein 36.5 g; Fiber 0 g; Sugar 12.5 g;

Fast Pork Meatballs with Red Chili

Prep T: 5 min | Cook T: 15 min | Servings: 4

Ingredients

- 454 grams of ground pork
- 2 cloves garlic, finely minced
- 128 grams scallions, finely chopped
- 1½ tbsp Worcestershire sauce
- ½ tsp freshly grated ginger root
- 1 tsp turmeric powder
- 1 tbsp oyster sauce
- 1 small sliced red chili, for garnish
- Cooking Spray

Directions

1. Spritz the air fry basket with cooking spray.
2. Put all the ingredients, except for the red chili in a large bowl. Toss to mix well.
3. Shape the mixture into equally sized balls, then arrange them in the air fry basket and spritz with cooking spray.
4. Place the basket on the air fry position.
5. Select Air Fry. Set temperature to 180 degs C and set time to 15 min.
6. After 7 min, remove the basket from the air fryer grill. Flip the balls. Return the basket to the air fryer grill and continue cooking.
7. When cooking is complete, the balls should be lightly browned.
8. Serve the pork meatballs with red chili on top.

Nutrition: Calories 307; Fat 24 g; Carbohydrates 2.5 g; Protein 19 g; Fiber 0.5 g; Sugar 0.8 g;

Pork, Squash, and Pepper Kebabs

Prep T: 1 hour 20 min | Cook T: 8 min | Servings: 4

Ingredients

For the Pork:

- 454 grams of pork steak, cut into cubes
- 1 tbsp white wine vinegar
- 3 tbsp steak sauce
- 32 grams soy sauce
- 1 tsp powdered chili
- 1 tsp red chili flakes
- 2 tsps smoked paprika
- 1 tsp garlic salt

For the Vegetable:

- 1 green squash, deseeded and cut into cubes
- 1 yellow squash, deseeded and cut into cubes
- 1 red pepper, cut into cubes
- 1 green pepper, cut into cubes
- Salt and ground black pepper, to taste
- Cooking Spray

Special Equipment:

- 4 bamboo skewers, soaked in water for at least 30 min

Directions

1. Combine the ingredients for the pork in a large bowl. Press the pork to dunk in the marinade. Wrap the bowl in plastic and let it rest in the refrigerator for at least an hour.
2. Spritz the air fry basket with cooking spray.
3. Remove the pork from the marinade and run the skewers through the pork and vegetables alternatively. Sprinkle with salt and pepper to taste.
4. Arrange the skewers in the pan and spritz with cooking spray.
5. Place the basket on the air fry position.
6. Select Air Fry. Set temperature to 193 degs C and set time to 8 min.
7. After 4 min, remove the basket from the air fryer grill. Flip the skewers. Return the basket to the air fryer grill and continue cooking.
8. When cooking is complete, the pork should be browned, and the vegetables should be lightly charred and tender.
9. Serve immediately.

Nutrition: Calories 240; Fat 13.5 g; Carbohydrates 5 g; Protein 20 g; Fiber 0.8 g; Sugar 3 g;

Lamb and Leeks

Prep T: 5 minutes | Cook T: 30 minutes | Servings: 4

Ingredients

- 453 grams of lamb shoulder, trimmed and cubed
- 2 tbsp olive oil
- 3 garlic cloves, minced
- 4 baby leeks, halved
- 128 grams okra
- 453 grams of tomatoes, peeled and chopped
- Salt and black pepper to the taste
- 1 tbsp tarragon, chopped

Directions

1. Heat up a pan that fits your air fryer with the oil over medium-high heat, add the lamb, garlic, salt and pepper, toss and brown for 5 minutes.
2. Add the remaining ingredients except the tarragon, toss, introduce the pan in the fryer and cook at 205 degs C for 25 minutes.

3. Divide everything into bowls and serve for lunch.

Nutrition: Calories: 235; Fat: 12g; Fiber: 4g; Carbs: 5g; Protein:15g

Herbed Roast Beef

Prep T: 10 min | Cook T: 15 min | Serving: 10-12

Ingredients

- 1/2 tsp. fresh rosemary
- 1 tsp. dried thyme
- 1/4 tsp. pepper
- 1 tsp. salt
- 1.8 kg of top round roast beef
- 2 tsp. olive oil

Directions

1. Ensure your air fryer is preheated to 182 degs C.
2. Rub olive oil all over beef.
3. Mix rosemary, thyme, pepper, and salt together and proceed to rub all sides of beef with spice mixture.
4. Place seasoned beef into air fryer and cook 20 min.
5. Allow roast to rest 10 min before slicing to serve.

Nutrition: Calories: 212; Sodium: 321 mg; Total Carbs: 14.6 g; Dietary Fiber: 4.4 g; Sugar: 8 g; Protein:17.3 g

Baked Ground Beef with Zucchini

Prep T: 5 min | Cook T: 12 min | Servings: 4

Ingredients

- 680 grams of ground beef
- 454 grams of chopped zucchini
- 2 tbsp extra-virgin olive oil
- 1 tsp dried oregano
- 1 tsp dried basil
- 1 tsp dried rosemary
- 2 tbsp fresh chives, chopped

Directions

1. In a large bowl, combine all the ingredients, except for the chives, until well blended.
2. Place the beef and zucchini mixture in the baking pan.
3. Place the pan on the bake position.
4. Select Bake, set temperature to 205 degs C and set time to 12 min.
5. When cooking is complete, the beef should be browned and the zucchini should be tender.
6. Divide the beef and zucchini mixture among four serving dishes. Top with fresh chives and serve hot.

Nutrition: Calories 415; Fat 28.5 g; Carbohydrates 3.3 g; Protein 34.4 g; Fiber 1 g; Sugar 3 g;

Paprika Pork Ribs

Prep T: 30 min | Cook T: 15 min | Servings: 2

Ingredients

- 453 grams of ribs, cut apart so they fit in the air fryer
- 11/2 tbsp paprika
- 21/2 tbsp olive oil
- 1 tsp salt

Directions

1. Place the ribs in a large bowl.
2. Pour in the paprika, olive oil and salt and stir around or mix with your hands to make sure the ribs are all coated.
3. Set the basket of the air fryer with cooking spray and place the coated ribs in.
4. Cook at 182 degs C – Do not preheat the air fryer! Cook for 20 min, removing the basket and shaking the ribs around 2 times during those 20 min.
5. They should be done and the meat should pull away from the bone.

Nutrition: Calories: 365; Fat: 18 g; Carbs: 5 g; Sugar: 2 g; Protein:40 g; Cholesterol: 0 mg

Lamb Rack with Pistachio

Prep T: 10 min | Cook T: 20 min | Servings: 2

Ingredients

- 64 grams finely chopped pistachios
- 1 tsp chopped fresh rosemary
- 3 tbsp panko breadcrumbs
- 2 tsps chopped fresh oregano
- 1 tbsp olive oil
- Salt and freshly ground black pepper, to taste
- 1 lamb rack, bones fat trimmed and frenched
- 1 tbsp Dijon mustard

Directions

1. Place the crisper tray on the air fry position. Select Air Fry, set the temperature to 193 degs C and set the time to 12 min.
2. Put the pistachios, rosemary, breadcrumbs, oregano, olive oil, salt, and black pepper in a food processor. Pulse to combine until smooth.
3. Rub the lamb rack with salt and black pepper on a clean work surface, then place it in the crisper tray.
4. Air fry for 12 min or until lightly browned. Flip the lamb halfway through the cooking time.

5. Transfer the lamb to a plate and brush with Dijon mustard on the fat side, then sprinkle with the pistachios mixture over the lamb rack to coat well.
6. Put the lamb rack back to the crisper tray. Air fry for 8 more min or until the internal temperature of the rack reaches at least 63 degs C.
7. Remove the lamb rack from the grill with tongs and allow to cool for 5 min before sling to serve.

Nutrition: Calories 260; Fat 12.5 g; Carbohydrates 19.5 g; Protein 14 g; Fiber 1 g; Sugar 1.5 g;

Teriyaki Pork and Mushroom Rolls

Prep T: 10 min | Cook T: 8 min | Servings: 6

Ingredients

- 4 tbsp brown sugar
- 4 tbsp mirin
- 4 tbsp soy sauce
- 1 tsp almond flour
- 5 cm ginger, chopped
- 452 grams of pork belly slices
- 170 grams of Enoki mushrooms

Directions

1. Mix the brown sugar, mirin, soy sauce, almond flour, and ginger together until brown sugar dissolves.
2. Take pork belly slices and wrap around a bundle of mushrooms. Brush each roll with teriyaki sauce. Chill for half an hour.
3. Place the crisper tray on the air fry position. Select Air Fry, set the temperature to 177 degs C and set the time to 8 min.
4. Add marinated pork rolls to the crisper tray.
5. Air fry for 8 min. Flip the rolls halfway through.
6. Serve immediately.

Nutrition: Calories 97; Fat 9 g; Carbohydrates 2.2 g; Protein 2 g; Fiber 0.6 g; Sugar 6 g;

Swedish Beef Meatballs

Prep T: 10 min | Cook T: 12 min | Servings: 8

Ingredients

- 454 grams of ground beef
- 1 egg, beaten
- 2 carrots, shredded
- 2 bread slices, crumbled
- 1 small onion, minced
- 1⁄2 tsps garlic salt
- Pepper and salt, to taste
- 128 grams tomato sauce
- 256 grams pasta sauce

Directions

1. Place the crisper tray on the air fry position. Select Air Fry, set the temperature to 204 degs C and set the time to 7 min.
2. In a bowl, combine the ground beef, egg, carrots, crumbled bread, onion, garlic salt, pepper, and salt.
3. Divide the mixture into equal amounts and shape each one into a small meatball.
4. Put them in the crisper tray. Air fry for 7 min.
5. Transfer the meatballs to a dish and top with the tomato sauce and pasta sauce. Set the dish into the pan and allow to air fry at 160 degs C for 5 more min. Serve hot.

Nutrition: Calories 140; Fat 6.7 g; Carbohydrates 6.9 g; Protein 11.2 g; Fiber 0.8 g; Sugar 4.5 g;

Air Fryer Burgers

Prep T: 10 min | Cook T: 10 min | Serving: 4

Ingredients

- 453 grams of lean ground beef
- 1 tsp. dried parsley
- 1/2 tsp. dried oregano
- 1/2 tsp. pepper
- 1/2 tsp. salt
- 1/2 tsp. onion powder
- 1/2 tsp. garlic powder
- Few drops of liquid smoke
- 1 tsp. Worcestershire sauce

Directions

1. Ensure your air fryer is preheated to 176 degs C.
2. Mix all seasonings together till combined.
3. Place beef in a bowl and add seasonings. Mix well, but do not over mix.
4. Make 4 patties from the mixture and using your thumb, making an indent in the center of each patty.
5. Add patties to air fryer basket and cook 10 min. No need to turn!

Nutrition: Calories: 346; Carbs: 9.8g; Protein:48.2g; Fat: 12.6g

Roasted Filet Mignon

Prep+ Cook T: 30 min | Servings:: 2

Ingredients

- 283 grams of filet mignon
- 1 tbsp. Italian herbs, chopped
- Salt & pepper
- 2 tbsp. olive oil

Directions

1. Preheat the Air Fryer to 200 degs C.
2. Mix all the seasonings with oil, and rub the mixture on the steak.
3. Roast it for 30 min.

Nutrition: Calories: 303; Fat: 19.5 g; Protein: 32 g

Fast Salsa Meatballs

Prep T: 10 min | Cook T: 10 min | Servings: 4

Ingredients

- 454 grams of ground beef (85% lean)
- 64 grams salsa
- 32 grams diced green or red bell peppers
- 1 large egg, beaten
- 32 grams chopped onions
- 1⁄2 tsp chili powder
- 1 clove garlic, minced
- 1⁄2 tsp ground cumin
- 1 tsp fine sea salt
- Lime wedges, for serving
- Cooking Spray

Directions

1. Spritz the air fry basket with cooking spray.
2. Combine all the ingredients in a large bowl. Stir to mix well.

3. Divide and shape the mixture into 2.5 cm balls. Arrange the balls in the basket and spritz with cooking spray.
4. Place the basket on the air fry position.
5. Select Air Fry. Set temperature to 180 degs C and set time to 10 min. Flip the balls with tongs halfway through.
6. When cooking is complete, the balls should be well browned.
7. Transfer the balls on a plate and squeeze the lime wedges over before serving.

Nutrition: Calories 250; Fat 15.5 g; Carbohydrates 2 g; Protein 23.5 g; Fiber 0.5 g; Sugar 1.25 g

Lamb Potato Chips Baked

Prep T: 10 min | Cook T: 25 min | Serving: 4

Ingredients

- 226 grams of minced lamb
- 1 tbsp. parsley chopped
- 2 tsp curry powder
- 1 pinch salt and black pepper
- 453 grams of potato cooked, mashed
- 29 grams of cheese grated
- 43 grams of potato chips crushed

Directions

1. Mix lamb, curry powder, seasoning and parsley.
2. Spread this lamb mixture in a casserole dish.
3. Top the lamb mixture with potato mash, cheese, and potato chips.
4. Choose "Power Button" of Air Fry Oven and select the "Bake" mode.
5. Choose the Time button and set the cooking time to 20 min.
6. Now press the Temp button and set the temperature at 176 degs C.
7. Once preheated, place casserole dish in the oven and close its lid.
8. Serve warm.

Nutrition: Calories: 301 ; Total Fat: 15.8 g; Total Carbs: 31.7 g ; Fiber: 0.3 g; Sugar: 0.1 g; Protein:28.2 g

Balsamic-Glazed Pork Chops

Prep T: 5 min | Cook T: 50| Servings: 4

Ingredients

- 96 grams balsamic vinegar
- 11/2 tbsp sugar
- 1 tbsp butter
- ½ tbsp olive oil
- ¼ tbsp salt
- 4 pork rib chops

Directions

1. Place all ingredients in a bowl and allow the meat to marinate in the fridge for at least 2 hours. Preheat the air fryer to 200 degs C. Place the grill pan accessory in the air fryer.
2. Grill the pork chops for 20 min making sure to flip the meat every 10 min for even grilling. Meanwhile, pour the balsamic vinegar into a saucepan and allow simmering for at least 10 min until the sauce thickens. Brush the meat with the glaze before serving.

Nutrition: Calories: 274; Fat: 18g; Protein: 17g; Carbs: 1.2 g;

Lamb Ribs with Fresh mint

Prep T: 5 min | Cook T: 18 min | Servings: 4

Ingredients

- 2 tbsp mustard
- 454 grams of lamb ribs
- 1 tsp rosemary, chopped
- Salt and ground black pepper, to taste
- 32 grams mint leaves, chopped
- 128 ml Greek yogurt

Directions

1. Place the crisper tray on the air fry position. Select Air Fry, set the temperature to (177 degs C and set the time to 18 min.
2. Use a brush to apply the mustard to the lamb ribs, and season with rosemary, salt, and pepper. Transfer to the crisper tray.
3. Air fry for 18 min.
4. Meanwhile, combine the mint leaves and yogurt in a bowl.
5. Remove the lamb ribs from the grill when cooked and serve with the mint yogurt.

*Nutrition: Calories **413**; Fat **35.5** g; Carbohydrates **2.3** g; Protein **19.5** g; Fiber **0.2** g; Sugar **1.2** g;*

Italian Steak and Spinach Rolls

Prep T: 50 min | Cook T: 9 min | Servings: 4

Ingredients

- 2 tsps dried Italian seasoning
- 2 cloves garlic, minced
- tbsp vegetable oil
- tsp kosher salt
- 1 tsp ground black pepper
- 454 grams of flank steak, 6 to 12 mm thick
- 284 grams of package frozen spinach, thawed and squeezed dry
- 64 grams diced jarred roasted red pepper
- 128 grams shredded Mozzarella cheese
- Cooking Spray

Directions

1. Combine the Italian seasoning, garlic, vegetable oil, salt, and ground black pepper in a large bowl. Stir to mix well.
2. Dunk the steak in the seasoning mixture and toss to coat well. Wrap the bowl in plastic and marinate under room temperature for at least 30 min.
3. Spritz the air fry basket with cooking spray.
4. Remove the marinated steak from the bowl and unfold on a clean work surface, then spread the top of the steak with a layer of spinach, a layer of red pepper and a layer of cheese. Leave a 6 mm edge uncovered.
5. Roll the steak up to wrap the filling, then secure with 3 toothpicks. Cut the roll in half and transfer the rolls in the prepared basket, seam side down.
6. Select Air Fry, Convection. Set temperature to 205 degs C and set time to 9 min. Press Start to begin preheating.
7. Once preheated, place the basket on the air fry position. Flip the rolls halfway through the cooking.
8. When cooking is complete, the steak should be lightly browned and the internal temperature reaches at least 63 degs C.
9. Detach the rolls from the oven and slice to serve.

Nutrition: Calories 259; Fat 10 g; Carbohydrates 16 g; Sugar 0 g; Protein 25 g; Cholesterol 0 mg;

Ginger-Orange Beef Strips

Prep T: 23 min | Cook T: 25 min | Servings: 3

Ingredients

- 680 grams of stir-fry steak slices
- 11/2 tsp. sesame oil
- 1 navel oranges, segmented
- 1 tbsp. olive oil
- 1 tbsp. rice vinegar
- 1 tsp. grated ginger
- 2 scallions, minced
- 3 cloves of garlic, diced
- 3 tbsp. molasses
- 3 tbsp. soy sauce
- 6 tbsp. cornstarch

Directions

1. Preheat the Air Fryer to 165 degs C. Season the steak slices with soy sauce and dust with cornstarch. Put in the Air Fryer basket and air fry for 25 min.
2. Meanwhile, place in the skillet oil and heat over medium flame. Sauté the garlic and ginger until fragrant. Stir in the oranges, molasses, and rice vinegar. Season with salt and pepper to taste.
3. Once the meat is done, place in the skillet and stir to coat the sauce. Drizzle with oil and garnish with scallions.

Nutrition: Calories 193; Fat 7 g; Carbohydrates 7 g; Sugar 0 g; Protein 25 g; Cholesterol 0 mg;

Balsamic London Broil

Prep T: 15 min | Cook T: 25 min | Servings: 8

Ingredients

- 907 grams of London broil
- 3 large garlic cloves, minced
- 3 tbsp balsamic vinegar
- 3 tbsp whole-grain mustard
- 2 tbsp olive oil
- Sea salt and ground black pepper, to taste
- 1⁄2 tsps dried hot red pepper flakes

Directions

1. Wash and dry the London broil. Score its sides with a knife.
2. Mix the remaining ingredients. Rub this mixture into the broil, coating it well. Allow marinating for a minimum of 3 hours.
3. Place the crisper tray on the air fry position. Select Air Fry, set the temperature to 204 degs C and set the time to 25 min.
4. Place the meat in the crisper tray. Air fry for 15 min. Turn it over and air fry for an additional 10 min before serving.

Nutrition: Calories 198; Fat 6.2 g; Carbohydrates 0.7 g; Protein 35 g ; Fiber 0.25 g; Sugar 0.1 g;

Beef Jerky

Prep T: 10 min | Cook T: 4 hours| Servings: 6

Ingredients

- 907 grams of London broil, sliced thinly
- 1 tsp. onion powder
- 3 tbsp. brown sugar
- 3 tbsp. soy sauce
- 1 tsp. olive oil
- 3/4 tsp. garlic powder

Directions

1. Add all ingredients except meat to the large zip-lock bag. Mix until well combined. Add meat to the bag. Seal bag and massage gently to cover the meat with marinade.
2. Let marinate the meat for 1 hour. Arrange marinated meat slices on an air fryer tray and dehydrate at 72 degs C for 4 hours. Serve.

Nutrition: Calories 133; Fat 4.7 g; Carbohydrates 9.4 g; Sugar 0 g; Protein 13.4 g; Cholesterol 0 mg;

Spiced Pork Shoulder

Prep T: 15 min | Cook T: 55 min | Servings: 6

Ingredients

- 1 tsp ground cumin

- 1 tsp cayenne pepper
- 1 tsp garlic powder
- Salt and ground black pepper, as required
- 907 grams of skin-on pork shoulder

Directions

1. Mix the spices, salt, and black pepper in a small bowl. Arrange the pork shoulder onto a cutting board, skin-side down.
2. Season the inner side of pork shoulder with salt and black pepper. With kitchen twines, tie the pork shoulder into a long round cylinder shape.
3. Season the outer side of pork shoulder with spice mixture. Insert the rotisserie rod through the pork shoulder. Insert the rotisserie forks, one on each side of the rod, to secure the pork shoulder.
4. Set your air fryer to 177 degs C, and then roast for 55 min. Remove the pork from the air fryer and place onto a platter for about 10 min before slicing. Cut the pork shoulder into desired sized slices using a sharp knife and serve.

Nutrition: Calories 445; Fat 32.5 g; Carbohydrates 0.7 g; Sugar 0 g; Protein 35.4 g; Cholesterol 0 mg;

Rib Eye Steak

Prep T: 15 min | Cook T: 22 min | Servings: 4

Ingredients

- 455 grams of Rib eye steak
- 1 tbsp. salt
- 3/4 tbsp. pepper
- 1/2 tbsp. garlic powder
- 3/4 steak seasoning

Directions

1. Season the steak with the spices and set aside.
2. Select the air fry setting. Set the temperature at 200 degs C for 12 min. Press start.
3. When the steak is halfway cooked, flip it.
4. Set the steak to a plate and cover it with a paper foil. Let it rest for 8 min before serving it.

Nutrition: Calories 330; Fat 24.5 g; Carbohydrates 0 g; Sugar 0 g; Protein 19.5 g;

Cheddar Beef Chili

Prep T: 15 minutes | Cook T: 20 minutes | Servings: 2

Ingredients

- 128 grams ground beef
- 32 grams Cheddar cheese, shredded
- 32 grams green beans, trimmed and halved
- 32 grams spring onion, diced
- 1 tsp fresh cilantro, chopped
- 2 chili pepper, chopped
- 1 tsp ghee
- 1 tbsp keto tomato sauce
- 64 grams chicken broth
- ½ tsp salt
- ¼ tsp garlic powder

Directions

1. Put ghee in the skillet and melt it. Put the ground beef in the skillet. Add spring onion, garlic powder, and salt. Stir the ground beef mixture and cook it over the medium heat for 5 minutes. Then transfer the mixture in the air fryer pan.

2. Add tomato sauce and stir until homogenous. Add chicken broth, chili peppers, and cilantro. Then add green beans and cilantro.
3. Mix up the chili gently and top with Cheddar cheese. Preheat the air fryer to 198 degs C. Put the pan with chili con carne in the air fryer and cook it for 10 minutes.

Nutrition: Calories: 244; Fat: 15.5g; Fiber: 1.7g; Carbs: 6.4g; Protein:19.4g

Italian Pork Meatballs

Prep T: 15 minutes | Cook T: 10 minutes | Servings: 4

Ingredients

- 340 grams of ground pork
- 57 grams of Parmesan, grated
- 1 tsp Italian seasonings
- 1 tsp ground black pepper
- 1 tsp chili flakes
- 1 tsp fresh parsley, chopped
- 1 tsp avocado oil
- 1 tsp salt

Directions

1. Mix up ground pork, Parmesan, Italian seasoning, ground black pepper, chili flakes, parsley, and salt. Make 4 balls from the mixture. Preheat the air fryer to 185 degs F. Then brush the air fryer basket with avocado oil.
2. Put the pork balls inside. Cook them at 185 degs C for 10 minutes.

Nutrition: Calories: 174; Fat: 6.6g; Fiber: 0.2g; Carbs: 1.1g; Protein:26.9g

Chapter 7: Fish and Seafood

Salmon Fillet with Tomatoes

Prep T: 10 min | Cook T: 15 min | Servings: 4

Ingredients

- 680 grams of salmon fillets, patted dry
- 1 tsp kosher salt, divided
- 2 pints cherry or grape tomatoes, halved if large, divided
- 3 tbsp extra-virgin olive oil, divided
- 2 garlic cloves, minced
- 1 small red bell pepper, deseeded and chopped
- 2 tbsp chopped fresh basil, divided

Directions

1. Season both sides of the salmon with 1/2 tsp of kosher salt.
2. Put about half of the tomatoes in a large bowl, along with 2 tbsp of olive oil, the remaining 1/2 tsp of kosher salt, bell pepper, garlic, and 1 tbsp of basil. Toss to coat and then transfer to the sheet pan.
3. Arrange the salmon fillets on the sheet pan, skin-side down. Brush them with the remaining 1 tbsp of olive oil.
4. Place the pan on the toast position.
5. Select Toast, set temperature to 190 degs C, and set time to 15 min.
6. After 7 min, remove the pan and fold in the remaining tomatoes. Return the pan to the air fryer grill and continue cooking.
7. When cooked, remove the pan from the air fryer grill. Serve sprinkled with the remaining 1 tbsp of basil.

Nutrition: Calories 312; Fat 19.5 g; Carbohydrates 2.3 g; Protein 30.3 g; Fiber 0.3 g; Sugar 1.8 g;

Cod Burgers

Prep T: 15 min | Cook T: 7 min | Servings: 6

Ingredients

- 227 grams of cod fillets
- 1/2 tsp fresh lime zest, grated finely
- 1/2 egg
- 1/2 tsp red chili paste
- Salt, to taste
- 1/2 tbsp fresh lime juice
- 3 tbsp coconut, grated and divided

- 1 small scallion, chopped finely
- 1 tbsp fresh parsley, chopped

Directions

1. In a food processor, add cod filets, lime zest, egg, chili paste, salt and lime juice and pulse until smooth.
2. Transfer the cod mixture into a bowl.
3. Add 11/2 tbsp coconut, scallion and parsley and mix until well combined.
4. Make 6 equal-sized patties from the mixture.
5. In a shallow dish, place the remaining coconut.
6. Coat the patties in coconut evenly.
7. Choose "Power Button" of Air Fry and select the "Air Fry" mode.
8. Choose the Time button and set the cooking time to 7 min.
9. Now press the Temp button and set the temperature at 190 degs C.
10. Press "Start/Pause" button to start.
11. After the Air Fryer is preheated, open the lid.
12. Arrange the patties in the greased air fryer basket and insert in the oven.
13. Serve hot.

Nutrition: Calories 56; Fat 1.6g; Protein 9.3g; Carbs: 2 g;

Broiled Crab Cakes With Herb Sauce

Prep T and Cook T: 25 min | Servings: 4

Ingredients

- 453 grams of crab meat
- 1 large egg
- 1 minced garlic clove
- 1/4 parsley, chopped
- 1 tsp. seafood seasoning
- Salt & pepper
- 1 shallot
- 1 tbsp. brown mustard
- 4 tbsp. mayo
- 1 tbsp. flour

Directions

1. Mix mayo, eggs, mustard, seasoning, and flour until smooth
2. Stir in the lump of crab meat along with shallots, parsley, garlic.

3.   Make 4 balls and place them on the pan
4.   Broil in the Air Fryer at 121 degs C for 8 min.

*Nutrition: Calories **169**; Fat **7** g; Carbohydrates **1.3** g; Protein **22.3** g; Fiber **0** g; Sugar **0.5** g;*

Golden Tuna Lettuce Wraps

Prep T: 10 min | Cook T: 4 to 7 min | Servings: 4

Ingredients

- 454 grams of fresh tuna steak, cut into 2.5 cm cubes
- 2 garlic cloves, minced
- 1 tbsp grated fresh ginger
- 1⁄2 tsp toasted sesame oil
- 4 low-sodium whole-wheat tortillas
- 256 grams shredded romaine lettuce
- 1 red bell pepper, thinly sliced
- 32 grams low-fat mayonnaise

Directions

1.   Combine the tuna cubes, ginger, garlic, and sesame oil in a medium bowl and toss until well coated. Allow sitting for 10 min.
2.   When ready, place the tuna cubes in the air fry basket.
3.   Place the basket on the air fry position.
4.   Select Air Fry, set temp to 199 degs C, and set time to 6 min.
5.   When cooking is complete, the tuna cubes should be cooked through and golden brown. Remove the tuna cubes from the air fryer grill to a plate.
6.   Make the wraps: Place the tortillas on a flat surface and top each tortilla evenly with the cooked tuna, lettuce, bell pepper, and finish with the mayonnaise. Roll them up and serve immediately.

Nutrition: Calories 292; Fat 14 g; Carbohydrates 12 g; Protein 27.3 g; Fiber 1.3 g; Sugar 0 g;

Butter Mussels

Prep T: 10 minutes | Cook T: 2 minutes | Servings:5

Ingredients

- 907 grams of mussels
- 1 shallot, chopped
- 1 tbsp minced garlic
- 1 tbsp butter, melted
- 1 tsp sunflower oil
- 1 tsp salt
- 1 tbsp fresh parsley, chopped
- ½ tsp chili flakes

Directions

1.   Clean and wash mussels and put them in the big bowl. Add shallot, minced garlic, butter, sunflower oil, salt, and chili flakes.
2.   Shake the mussels well. Preheat the air fryer to 198 degs C.
3.   Put the mussels in the air fryer basket and cook for 2 minutes. Then transfer the cooked meal in the serving bowl and top it with chopped fresh parsley.

Nutrition: Calories: 192; Fat: 7.3g; Fiber: 0.1g; Carbs: 8.3g; Protein:21.9g

Grilled Swordfish Steaks

Prep T: 5 min | Cook T: 8 min | Servings: 4

Ingredients

- 1 tbsp freshly squeezed lemon juice
- 1 tbsp extra-virgin olive oil
- Sea salt, to taste
- Freshly ground black pepper, to taste
- 908 grams of fresh swordfish steaks, about 2.5 cm thick
- 4 tbsp unsalted butter
- 1 lemon, sliced crosswise into 8 slices
- 2 tbsp capers, drained

Directions

1.   Get a bowl and mix the lemon juice and oil in it. Season the swordfish steaks with salt and pepper on each side, and place them in the oil mixture. Turn to coat both sides. Refrigerate for 15 min.
2.   Place the grill plate on the grill position. Select Grill, set the temperature to 232 degs C, and set the time to 8 min.
3.   Place the swordfish on the grill plate. Grill for 9 min. (There is no need to flip the swordfish during cooking.)
4.   While the swordfish grills, melt the butter in a small saucepan over medium heat. Stir and grill for about 3 min, until the butter has slightly browned. Add the lemon slices and capers to the pan, and grill for 1 minute. Turn off the heat.
5.   Remove the swordfish from the grill and transfer it to a cutting board. Slice the fish into thick strips, transfer to serving platter, pour the caper sauce over the top, and serve immediately.

Nutrition: Calories 455; Fat 29.3 g; Carbohydrates 0 g; Protein 44 g; Fiber 0 g; Sugar 0 g;

Garlic Shrimp Mix

Prep T: 10 minutes | Cook T: 5 minutes | Servings: 3

Ingredients

- 453 grams of shrimps, peeled
- ½ tsp garlic powder
- ¼ tsp minced garlic
- 1 tsp ground cumin
- ¼ tsp lemon zest, grated
- ½ tbsp avocado oil
- ½ tsp dried parsley

Directions

1. In the mixing bowl mix up shrimps, garlic powder, minced garlic, ground cumin, lemon zest, and dried parsley. Then add avocado oil and mix up the shrimps well.
2. Preheat the air fryer to 205 degs C. Put the shrimps in the preheated air fryer basket and cook for 5 minutes.

Nutrition: Calories: 187; Fat: 3g; Fiber: 0.2g; Carbs: 3.2g; Protein:34.7g

Spiced Crab Cakes

Prep T: 10 min | Cook T: 10 min | Servings: 4

Ingredients

- 1 egg
- 64 grams mayonnaise, plus 3 tbsp
- Juice of 1/2 lemon
- 1 tbsp minced scallions (green parts only)
- 1 tsp Old Bay seasoning
- 227 grams of lump crab meat
- Nonstick cooking spray
- 1/2 tsp cayenne pepper
- 1/4 tsp paprika
- 1/4 tsp garlic powder
- 1/4 tsp chili powder
- 1/4 tsp onion powder
- 1/4 tsp freshly ground black pepper
- 1/8 tsp ground nutmeg

Directions

1. Place the crisper tray on the air fry position. Select Air Fry, set the temperature to 191 degs C, and set the time to 10 min.
2. In a medium bowl, whisk together the egg, 3 tbsp of mayonnaise, lemon juice, scallions, and Old Bay seasoning. Gently stir in the crab meat, making sure not to break up the meat into small pieces. Add the breadcrumbs, and gradually mix them in. Form the mixture into four patties.
3. Place the crab cakes in the crisper tray and coat them with the cooking spray. Air fry for 10 min.

4. While the crab cakes are cooking in a small bowl, mix the remaining 64 grams of mayonnaise, cayenne pepper, paprika, garlic powder, chili powder, onion powder, black pepper, and nutmeg until fully combined.
5. When cooking is complete, serve the crab cakes with the Cajun aioli spooned on top.

Nutrition: Calories 204; Fat 13.3 g; Carbohydrates 5.8 g; Protein 12.6 g; Fiber 1 g; Sugar 1 g;

Cajun Shrimps

Prep T: 10 minutes | Cook T: 6 minutes | Servings: 4

Ingredients

- 228 grams of shrimps, peeled
- 1 tsp Cajun spices
- 1 tsp cream cheese
- 1 egg, beaten
- ½ tsp salt
- 1 tsp avocado oil

Directions

1. Sprinkle the shrimps with Cajun spices and salt. In the mixing bowl mix up cream cheese and egg, Dip every shrimp in the egg mixture.
2. Preheat the air fryer to 205 degs C. Place the shrimps in the air fryer and sprinkle with avocado oil. Cook the popcorn shrimps for 6 minutes. Shake them well after 3 minutes of cooking.

Nutrition: Calories: 88; Fat: 2.5g; Fiber: 0.1g; Carbs: 1g; Protein:14.4g

Gold Salmon Patties

Prep T: 5 min | Cook T: 11 min | Makes 6 patties

Ingredients

- 418 grams of can pink salmon, drained and bones removed
- 64 grams bread crumbs
- 1 egg, whisked
- 2 scallions, diced
- 1 tsp garlic powder
- Salt and pepper, to taste
- Cooking Spray

Directions

1. Stir together the salmon, bread crumbs, whisked egg, garlic powder, scallions, salt, and pepper in a large bowl until well incorporated.

2. Divide the salmon mixture into six equal portions and form each into a patty with your hands.
3. Arrange the salmon patties in the air fry basket and spritz them with cooking spray.
4. Place the basket on the air fry position.
5. Air Fry, set the temperature to 205 degs C, and set time to 10 min. Flip the patties once halfway through.
6. When cooking is complete, the patties should be golden brown and cooked through. Remove the patties from the air fryer grill and serve on a plate.

Nutrition: Calories 142; Fat 7.8 g; Carbohydrates 9.5 g; Protein 23 g; Fiber 0.5 g; Sugar 0.8 g;

Crispy Fish Sticks

Prep T: 10 min | Cook T: 10 min | Servings: 4

Ingredients

- 454 grams of cod fillets
- 32 grams all-purpose flour
- 1 large egg
- 1 tsp Dijon mustard
- 64 grams bread crumbs
- 1 tbsp dried parsley
- 1 tsp paprika
- 1/2 tsp freshly ground black pepper
- Nonstick cooking spray

Directions

1. Place the crisper tray on the air fry position. Select Air Fry, set the temperature to 199 degs C, and set the time to 10 min.
2. Cut the fish fillets into 19 - to 25-mm-wide strips.
3. Place the flour on a plate. In a medium shallow bowl, whisk together the egg and Dijon mustard. In a separate medium shallow bowl, combine the bread crumbs, dried parsley, paprika, and black pepper.
4. One at a time, dredge the cod strips in the flour, shaking off any excess, then coat them in the egg mixture. Finally, dredge them in the bread crumb mixture and coat on all sides.
5. Spray the crisper tray with the cooking spray. Place the cod fillet strips in the crisper tray, and coat them with the cooking spray. Air fry for 10 min.
6. Remove the fish sticks from the crisper tray and serve.

Nutrition: Calories 187; Fat 2.5 g; Carbohydrates 13.5 g; Protein 24.5 g; Fiber 1 g; Sugar 0.8 g;

Panko-Crusted Catfish Nuggets

Prep T: 10 min | Cook T: 7 to 8 min | Servings: 4

Ingredients

- 2 medium catfish fillets, cut into chunks (approximately 5 cm)
- Salt and pepper, to taste
- 2 eggs
- 2 tbsp skim milk
- 64 grams cornstarch
- 128 grams panko bread crumbs
- Cooking Spray

Directions

1. In a medium bowl, season the fish chunks with salt and pepper to taste.
2. In a small bowl, beat together the eggs with milk until well combined.
3. Place the cornstarch and bread crumbs into separate shallow dishes.
4. Dredge the fish chunks one at a time in the cornstarch, coating well on both sides, then dip in the egg mixture, shaking off any excess, finally press well into the bread crumbs. Spritz the fish chunks with cooking spray.
5. Arrange the fish chunks in the air fry basket in a single layer.
6. Place the basket on the air fry position.
7. Select Air Fry, set the temperature to 199 degs C, and set time to 8 min. Flip the fish chunks halfway through the cooking time.
8. When cooking is complete, they should be no longer translucent in the center and golden brown. Remove the fish chunks from the air fryer grill to a plate. Serve warm.

Nutrition: Calories 310; Fat 7.8 g; Carbohydrates 34 g; Protein 22.5 g; Fiber 1 g; Sugar 1.5 g;

Panko Scallops

Prep T: 5 min | Cook T: 7 min | Servings: 4

Ingredients

- 1 egg
- 3 tbsp flour
- 128 grams bread crumbs
- 454 grams of fresh scallops
- 2 tbsp olive oil
- Salt and black pepper, to taste

Directions

1. In a bowl, lightly beat the egg. Place the flour and bread crumbs into separate shallow dishes.
2. Dredge the scallops in the flour and shake off any excess. Dip the flour-coated scallops in the beaten egg and roll in the bread crumbs.
3. Brush the scallops generously with olive oil and season with salt and pepper. Transfer the scallops to the air fry basket.
4. Place the basket on the air fry position.
5. Select Air Fry, set temperature to 182 degs C, and set time to 7 min. Flip the scallops halfway through the cooking time.
6. When cooking is complete, the scallops should reach an internal temperature of just 63 degs C on a meat thermometer. Remove the basket from the air fryer grill. Let the scallops cool for 5 min and serve.

Nutrition: Calories 226; Fat 2.7 g; Carbohydrates 26.5 g; Protein 19.5 g; Fiber 1.3 g; Sugar 1.5 g;

Fried Shrimp with Mayonnaise Sauce

Prep T: 5 min | Cook T: 7 min | Servings: 4

Ingredients

Shrimp:
- 12 jumbo shrimp
- 1/2 tsp garlic salt
- 1/4 tsp freshly cracked mixed peppercorns

Sauce:
- 4 tbsp mayonnaise
- 1 tsp grated lemon rind
- 1 tsp Dijon mustard
- 1 tsp chipanle powder
- 1/2 tsp cumin powder

Directions

1. Place the crisper tray on the air fry position. Select Air Fry, set the temperature to 202 degs C, and set the time to 7 min.
2. In a medium bowl, season the shrimp with garlic salt and cracked mixed peppercorns.

3. Place the shrimp in the crisper tray. Air fry for 5 min. Flip the shrimp and cook for another 2 min until they are pink and no longer opaque.
4. Meanwhile, stir together all the ingredients for the sauce in a small bowl until well mixed.
5. Remove the shrimp from the crisper tray and serve alongside the sauce.

Nutrition: Calories 152; Fat 6.5 g; Carbohydrates 0 g; Protein 22.5 g; Fiber 0 g; Sugar 0 g;

Creamy Salmon

Prep T: 15 min | Cook T: 20 min | Servings: 2

Ingredients

- Chopped dill (1 tbsp)
- Salt (1 pinch)
- Olive oil (1 tbsp)
- Natural yogurt (49 ml)
- Sour cream (3 tbsp)
- Salmon (340 grams - 6 pieces)

Directions

1. Heat the air fryer to 141 degs C.
2. Shake the salt over the salmon and add it to the basket with a spritz of olive oil.
3. Set the timer to air fry for ten min.
4. Whip the yogurt with the dill and salt.
5. Serve the salmon with the sauce to taste.

Nutrition: Calories: 239; Protein: 26.8 g; Fat: 13.7 g; Net Carbs: 2.6 g;

Lobster Tails with Green Olives

Prep T: 10 min| Cook T: 7 min| Servings: 5

Ingredients

- 907 grams of fresh lobster tails, cleaned and halved, in shells
- One tsp onion powder
- One tsp cayenne pepper
- Two garlic cloves, minced
- 128 grams of green olives

Directions

1. Warm the air fryer to 199 degs C and spray the basket with cooking spray.
2. Put all the ingredients except for the green olives in a sealable plastic bag. Seal the bag and shake until the lobster tails are coated completely.
3. Arrange the coated lobster tails in the greased basket. Cook in batches in the preheated air fryer for 6 to 7 min, shaking the basket halfway through.
4. Remove from the basket and serve with green olives.

Nutrition: Calories: 188 Fat: 6.8gCarbs: 1.9g Protein: 30.3g

Coconut Calamari

Prep T: 10 minutes | Cook T: 6 minutes | Servings: 2

Ingredients

- 170 grams of calamari, trimmed
- 2 tbsp coconut flakes
- 1 egg, beaten
- 1 tsp Italian seasonings
- Cooking Spray

Directions

1. Slice the calamari into the rings and sprinkle them with Italian seasonings. Then transfer the calamari rings in the bowl with a beaten egg and stir them gently. After this, sprinkle the calamari rings with coconut flakes and shake well.
2. Preheat the air fryer to 205 degs C. Put the calamari rings in the air fryer basket and spray them with cooking spray.
3. Cook the meal for 3 minutes. Then gently stir the calamari and cook them for 3 minutes more.

Nutrition: Calories: 135; Fat: 5.6g; Fiber: ,0.5g ; Carbs: 4.2g; Protein:18.1g

Lemon Shrimp and Zucchinis

Prep T: 5 minutes | Cook T: 15 minutes | Servings: 4

Ingredients

- 453 grams of shrimp, peeled and deveined
- A pinch of salt and black pepper
- zucchinis, cut into medium cubes
- 1 tbsp lemon juice
- 1 tbsp olive oil
- 1 tbsp garlic, minced

Directions

1. In a pan that fits the air fryer, combine all the ingredients, toss, put the pan in the machine and cook at 188 degs C for 15 minutes.
2. Divide between plates and serve right away.

Nutrition: Calories: 221; Fat: 9g; Fiber: 2g; Carbs: 15g; Protein:11g

Snapper Scampi

Prep T: 5 min | Cook T: 10 min | Servings: 4

Ingredients

- 4 (170 grams) skinless snapper or arctic char fillets
- 1 tbsp olive oil
- 3 tbsp lemon juice, divided
- 1/2 tsp dried basil
- Pinch salt
- Freshly ground black pepper
- 2 tbsp butter
- 2 cloves garlic, minced

Directions

1. Massage the fish fillets with olive oil and 1 tbsp of the lemon juice. Sprinkle with the basil, salt, and pepper, and place in the air fryer basket.
2. Grill the fish for 7 to 8 min or until the fish just flakes when tested with a fork. Remove the fish from the basket and put on a serving plate. Cover to keep warm.
3. In a 15-by-15-by-5-cm pan, combine the butter, remaining 2 tbsp lemon juice, and garlic. Cook in the air fryer for 1 to 2 min or until the garlic is sizzling. Pour this mixture over the fish and serve.

Nutrition: Calories: 265; Total Fat: 11g; Saturated Fat: 5g; Cholesterol: 109mg; Sodium: 215mg; Carbohydrates: 1g; Fiber: 0g; Protein: 39g;

Crispy Air Fried Halibut

Prep T: 10 min | Cook T: 40 min | Servings: 4

Ingredients

- Fresh chives (32 grams)
- Fresh parsley (64 grams)
- Fresh dill (32 grams)
- Black pepper and sea salt (to taste)
- Pork rinds (96 grams)
- Lemon zest (1 tbsp)
- Halibut fillets (4)
- Olive oil (1 tbsp)

Directions

1. Heat the air fryer to reach 199 degs C.
2. Chop the chives, dill, and parsley. Prepare the lemon zest until it is finely grated. Combine all the dry ingredients: parsley, pork rinds, chives, lemon zest, dill, black pepper, sea salt, and olive oil.
3. Rinse the halibut thoroughly and drain it on a layer of absorbent paper.
4. Prepare a baking sheet that fits into the pot. Pour the peel over the fish and press well.
5. Add the prepared fillets to the fryer basket to cook for 1/2 hour to serve.

Nutrition: Calories: 226; Protein: 9.2 g; Fat: 20.5 g; Net Carbs: 1.2 g;

Shrimp Salad with Caesar Dressing

Prep T: 10 min | Cook T: 15 min | Servings: 4

Ingredients

- 1/2 baguette, cut into 2.5 cm cubes (about 264 gramss)
- 4 tbsp extra-virgin olive oil, divided
- 1/4 tsp granulated garlic
- 1/4 tsp kosher salt
- 96 grams Caesar dressing, divided
- 2 romaine lettuce hearts, cut in half lengthwise and ends trimmed
- 454 grams of medium shrimp, peeled and deveined
- 57 grams of Parmesan cheese, coarsely grated

Directions

1. Make the croutons: Put the bread cubes in a medium bowl and drizzle 3 tbsp of olive oil over top. Season with salt and granulated garlic and toss to coat. Transfer to the air fry basket in a single layer.
2. Place the basket on the air fry position.
3. Select Air Fry, set temperature to 205 degs C, and set time to 4 min. Toss the croutons halfway through the cooking time.

4. When done, remove the air fry basket from the air fryer grill and set aside.
5. Brush 2 tbsp of Caesar dressing on the cut side of the lettuce. Set aside.
6. Toss the shrimp with the 32 grams of Caesar dressing in a large bowl until well coated. Set aside.
7. Coat the sheet pan with the remaining 1 tbsp of olive oil. Arrange the romaine halves on the coated pan, cut side down. Brush the tops with the remaining 2 tbsp of Caesar dressing.
8. Place the pan on the toast position.
9. Select Toast, set temperature to 190 degs C, and set time to 10 min.
10. After 5 min, remove the pan from the air fryer grill and flip the romaine halves. Spoon the shrimp around the lettuce. Return the pan to the air fryer grill and continue cooking.
11. When done, remove the sheet pan from the air fryer grill. If they are not quite cooked through, roast for another 1 minute.
12. On each of four plates, put a romaine half. Divide the shrimp among the plates and top with croutons and grated Parmesan cheese. Serve immediately.

Nutrition: Calories 286; Fat 17.5 g; Carbohydrates 6.8 g; Protein 25.5 g; Fiber 0.8 g; Sugar 0.3 g;

Beery Cod Fillet

Prep T: 5 min | Cook T: 15 min | Servings: 4

Ingredients

- 2 eggs
- 128 grams malty beer
- 128 grams all-purpose flour
- 64 grams cornstarch
- 1 tsp garlic powder
- Salt and pepper, to taste
- 452 grams of cod fillets
- Cooking Spray

Directions

1. In a shallow bowl, beat together the eggs with the beer. In another shallow bowl, thoroughly combine the cornstarch and flour. Sprinkle with salt, garlic powder, and pepper.
2. Dredge each cod fillet in the flour mixture, then in the egg mixture. Dip each piece of fish in the flour mixture a second time.
3. Spritz the air fry basket with cooking spray. Arrange the cod fillets in the basket in a single layer.

4. Place the basket on the air fry position.
5. Select Air Fry, set the temperature to 205 degs C, and set time to 15 min. Flip the fillets halfway through the cooking time.
6. When cooking is complete, the cod should reach an internal temperature of 63 degs C on a meat thermometer and the outside should be crispy. Let the fish cool for 5 min and serve.

Nutrition: Calories 310; Fat 4.8 g; Carbohydrates 33.8 g; Protein 30 g; Fiber 33.8 g; Sugar 0 g;

Air-Fried Sardines

Prep T: 10 min| Cook T: 12 min| Servings: 4
Ingredients

- 680 grams of sardines, rinsed and patted dry
- 1 tbsp lemon juice
- 1 tbsp Italian seasoning mix

Directions

1. Warm the air fryer to 180 degs C.
2. In a large bowl, merge the sardines with olive oil, lemon juice, Italian seasoning mix, soy sauce, salt, and pepper. Let the sardines marinate for 30 min.
3. Put the marinated sardines in the air fryer basket and air fry for about 12 min until flaky, flipping the fish halfway through.
4. Transfer to a plate and serve hot.

Nutrition: Calories: 438; Fat: 26.3g; Carbs: 3.6g; Protein: 42.6g;

Cod Sticks

Prep T: 15 minutes | Cook T: 6 minutes | Servings: 2

Ingredients

- 283 grams of cod fillet
- 32 grams almond flour
- 1 tbsp coconut flour
- 1 egg white
- 1 tsp dried oregano
- ½ tsp onion powder
- ½ tsp salt
- 1 tsp avocado oil

Directions

1. Chop the cod fillet and put it in the blender. Add coconut flour, egg white, dried oregano, salt, and onion powder. Blend the mixture until smooth.
2. Then make the medium sticks from the fish mixture and coat them in the almond flour. Brush the air fryer basket with avocado oil. Then place the cod sticks in the air fryer in one layer.
3. Cook the fish sticks for 6 minutes at 205 degs C. Flip the fish sticks after 3 minutes of cooking.

Nutrition: Calories: 167; Fat: 4.1g; Fiber: 2.3g; Carbs: 4.2g; Protein:28.8g

Apple Fritters

Prep/Cook T: 25 min | Servings: 4

Ingredients

- cooking spray
- 1 cup all-purpose flour
- ¼ cup white sugar
- ¼ cup milk
- 1 egg
- 1½ tsps baking powder
- 1 pinch salt
- 2 tbsp white sugar
- ½ teaspoon ground cinnamon
- 1 apple - peeled, cored, and chopped

Glaze:

- ½ cup confectioners' sugar
- 1 tablespoon milk
- ½ teaspoon caramel extract
- ¼ tsp ground cinnamon

Directions

1. Preheat an air fryer to 175 degs C. Place a parchment paper round into the bottom of the air fryer. Spray with nonstick cooking spray. Mix flour, 1/4 cup sugar, milk, egg, baking powder, and salt together in a small bowl. Stir until combined.
2. Mix 2 tbsp sugar with cinnamon in another bowl and sprinkle over apples until coated. Mix apples into the flour mixture until combined. Drop fritters using a cookie scoop onto the bottom of the air fryer basket.
3. Air-fry in the preheated fryer for 5 min utes. Flip fritters and cook until golden, about 5 min more.
4. Meanwhile, mix confectioners' sugar, milk, caramel extract, and cinnamon together in a bowl.
5. Transfer fritters to a cooling rack and drizzle with glaze.

Nutrition: 297 calories; protein 5.5g; carbohydrates 64.9g, fat 2.1

Caprese cake

Prep T: 20 min | Cook T: 25 min | Servings: 4

Ingredients

- 3 eggs
- 100 grams of sugar
- 220 grams of flour
- 30 grams of cocoa
- 50 ml of milk
- 40 grams of sunflower oil
- 8 g of baking powder
- 100 grams of whole peeled almonds
- 1 oven pan of 22 cm

Directions

1. In a planetary mixer or with an electric whisk, whip the eggs. Add the oil and milk slowly. At reduced speed, incorporate the flour, the sifted yeast, and cocoa.
2. Pour the mixture into the greased pan and sprinkle with almonds. Cook in the preheated air fryer at 160 degs C for 15 min and then raising the temperature to 185 degs C for another 10 min. Try with a stick to be sure of cooking.
3. Cool and serve with whipped cream or ice cream.

Nutrition: Calories 181; Fat 9 g; Carbohydrates 6 g; Sugar 4 g; Protein 3 g; Cholesterol 0 mg;

Lemony Cheesecake

Prep T: 5 min | Cook T: 25 min | Servings: 6

Ingredients

- 496 grams of ricotta cheese
- 153 grams of sugar
- 3 eggs, beaten
- 3 tbsp flour
- 1 lemon, juiced and zested
- 2 tsps vanilla extract

Directions

1. In a very large mixing bowl, stir all the ingredients until the mixture reaches a creamy consistency.
2. Pour the mixture in a baking pan and place it in the air fryer grill.
3. Place the pan on the bake position.
4. Select Bake, set temperature to 160 degs C, and set time to 25 min.
5. When cooking is complete, a toothpick inserted in the center should come out clean.
6. Allow to cool for 10 min on a wire rack before serving.

Nutrition: Calories 292.5; Fat 13.3 g; Carbohydrates 29.5 g; Protein 13.3 g; Fiber 0.4 g; Sugar 24.3 g;

Chocolate cookies "Biscotti al cioccolato"

Prep T: 20 min | Cook T: 5 min | Servings: 4

Ingredients

- 60 grams of cocoa powder
- 200 grams of brown sugar
- 125 grams of flour
- 60 grams of dark chocolate in small pieces
- 2 tsps of vanilla baking powder
- 1 pinch of salt
- 50 grams of butter at room temperature
- Baking paper

Directions

1. Mix the ingredients until a homogeneous mixture is obtained
2. Cut into balls and press them lightly to obtain some circles of approx. 5 cm in diameter.
3. Preheat the fryer to 200 degs C.
4. Place the cookies on the parchment paper 2.5 cm apart and bake
5. Lowering the temperature to 185 degs C for 5-6 min.

Nutrition: Calories 245; Fat 1 g; Carbohydrates 5 g; Sugar 1 g; Protein 13 g; Cholesterol 0 mg;

Chocolate Donuts

Prep T: 5 min | Cook T: 20 min |Serving: 8-10

Ingredients

- 226 grams of can jumbo biscuits
- Cooking oil
- Chocolate sauce

Directions

1. Separate the biscuit dough into eight biscuits and place them on a flat work surface. Use a small circle cookie cutter or a biscuit cutter to cut a hole in each biscuit center. You can also cut the holes using a knife.
2. Spray the air fryer basket with cooking oil.
3. Place four donuts in the air fryer oven. Do not stack. Spray with cooking oil. Set temperature to 177 degs C. Cook for 4 min.
4. Open the air fryer and flip the donuts. Cook for an additional 4 min.
5. Remove the cooked donuts from the air fryer oven, and then repeat for the remaining four donuts.
6. Drizzle chocolate sauce over the donuts and enjoy while warm.

Nutrition: Calories: 181; Fat: 98g; Protein: 3g; Fiber: 1g;

Brownies

Prep T: 10 minutes | Cook T: 25 minutes | Servings: 6

Ingredients

- 6 tbsp cream cheese, soft
- 3 eggs, whisked
- 1 tbsp cocoa powder
- 1 tbsp coconut oil, melted
- 32 grams almond flour

- 32 grams coconut flour
- ¼ tsp baking soda
- 1 tsp vanilla extract
- 64 grams almond milk
- 3 tbsp swerve
- Cooking Spray

Directions

1. Grease a cake pan that fits the air fryer with the cooking spray. In a bowl, mix rest of the ingredients, whisk well and pour into the pan.
2. Put the pan in your air fryer, cook at 188 degs C for 25 minutes, cool the brownies down, slice and serve.

Nutrition: Calories: 182; Fat: 12g; Fiber: 2g; Carbs: 4g; Protein:6g

Blueberry Crumble

Prep T: 15 min | Cook T: 15 min | Servings: 4

Ingredients

- 64 grams blueberries, sliced
- 1 apple, diced
- 2 tbsp butter
- 2 tbsp sugar
- 32 grams rice flour
- 1⁄2 tsp cinnamon powder

Directions

1. Mix all the ingredients in a tiny baking pan.
2. Place inside the air fryer.
3. Choose bake setting.
4. Set it to 177 degs C.
5. Cook for 15 min.

Serving Suggestions: Drizzle with honey before serving.

Prep & Cooking Tips: You can also use strawberries in place of blueberries.

Nutrition: Calories 118; Fat 5.7 g; Carbohydrates 15.8 g; Protein 0.5 g; Fiber 1 g; Sugar 8 g;

Vanilla Yogurt Cake

Prep T: 5 minutes | Cook T: 30 minutes | Servings: 12

Ingredients

- 6 eggs, whisked
- 1 tsp vanilla extract
- 1 tsp baking powder
- 255 grams of coconut flour
- 4 tbsp stevia

- 226 ml of Greek yogurt

Directions

1. In a bowl, mix all the ingredients and whisk well.
2. Pour this into a cake pan that fits the air fryer lined with parchment paper, put the pan in the air fryer and cook at 165 degs C for 30 minutes.

Nutrition: Calories: 181; Fat: 13g; Fiber: 2g; Carbs: 4g; Protein:5g

Air Fryer Beignets

Prep Time: 25 min s | Servings: 7

Ingredients

- cooking spray
- 1⁄2 cup all-purpose flour
- 32 grams white sugar
- 16 ml water
- 1 large egg, separated
- 1.1⁄2 teaspoons melted butter
- 1⁄2 teaspoon baking powder
- 1⁄2 tsp vanilla extract
- 1 pinch salt
- 2 tbsp confectioners' sugar, or to taste

Directions

1. Preheat air fryer to 185 degs C.
2. Spray a silicone egg-bite mold with nonstick cooking spray.
3. Whisk flour, sugar, water, egg yolk, butter, baking powder, vanilla extract, and salt together in a large bowl. Stir to combine.
4. Beat egg white in a small bowl using an electric hand mixer on medium speed until soft peaks form. Fold into batter. Add batter to the prepared mold using a small hinged ice cream scoop.
5. Place filled silicone mold into the basket of the air fryer.
6. Fry in the preheated air fryer for 10 minutes. Remove mold from the basket carefully; pop beignets out and flip over onto a parchment paper round.
7. Place parchment round with beignets back into the air fryer basket. Cook for an additional 4 min.
8. Remove beignets from the air fryer basket and dust with confectioners' sugar.

Nutrition: Calories: 72; Fat: 1.4 g; Fiber: 2g; Carbs: 9.5 g; Protein:5 g; Sugar: 6.5 g

Almond Cookies

Prep T: 5 minutes | Cook T: 15 minutes | Servings: 8

Ingredients

- 192 grams almonds, crushed
- 2 tbsp erythritol
- 1⁄2 tsp baking powder
- 1⁄4 tsp almond extract
- 2 eggs, whisked

Directions

1. In a bowl, mix all the ingredients and whisk well. Scoop 8 servings of this mix on a baking sheet that fits the air fryer which you've lined with parchment paper.
2. Put the baking sheet in your air fryer and cook at 176 degs C for 15 minutes. Serve cold.

Nutrition: Calories: 125; Fat: 7g; Fiber: 1g; Carbs: 5g; Protein:4g

Classic Pound Cake

Prep T: 5 min | Cook T: 30 min | Servings: 8

Ingredients

- 1 stick butter, at room temperature
- 128 grams Swerve
- 4 eggs
- 192 grams coconut flour
- 64 grams buttermilk
- 1⁄2 tsp baking soda
- 1⁄2 tsp baking powder
- 1⁄4 tsp salt
- 1 tsp vanilla essence
- A pinch of ground star anise
- A pinch of freshly grated nutmeg
- Cooking Spray

Directions

1. Place the baking pan on the bake position. Select Bake, set the temperature to 160 degs C, and set the time to 30 min.
2. Spray the baking pan with cooking spray.
3. With an electric or hand mixer, beat butter and Swerve until creamy. One at a time, mix in the eggs and whisk until fluffy. Add now the remaining ones and stir to combine.

4. Transfer the batter to the baking pan. Bake for 30 min until the center of the cake is springy. Rotate halfway through the cooking time.
5. Let the cake to cool down in the pan for 10 min before removing and serving.

Nutrition: Calories: 155; Fat: 12 g; Fiber: 0 g; Carbs:4 g; Protein:5.6 g; Sugar: 3.6 g

Air Fryer Apple Pies

Prep T: 10 min | Cook T: 25 min |Serving: 4
Ingredients

- 4 tbsp butter
- 6 tbsp brown sugar
- 1 tsp ground cinnamon
- 2 medium Granny Smith apples, diced
- 1 tsp cornstarch
- 2 tsp cold water
- 396 grams package pastry to get a 22 cm double-crust pie
- cooking spray
- 1/2 tbsp grape seed oil
- 32 grams powdered sugar
- 1 tsp milk, or more as required

Directions

1. Combine apples, butter, brown sugar, and cinnamon in a skillet. Cook over moderate heat until apples have softened, about 5 min.
2. Dissolve corn-starch in cold water. Stir into apple mixture and cook until sauce thickens about 1 min. Eliminate apple pie filling from heat and set aside to cool while you prepare the crust.
3. Unroll the pie crust onto a lightly floured surface and roll out slightly to smooth the dough's surface. Cut the dough into rectangles small enough so that two can fit on your air fryer simultaneously. Repeat with remaining crust until you've got eight equal rectangles, re-rolling a few of the bits of dough if necessary.
4. Wet the outer borders of 4 rectangles with water and then put some apple filling at the middle about 12 mm in the edges. Roll out the rest rectangles, so they are slightly more significant than the ones that are served. Put these rectangles in addition to the filling; crimp the edges with a fork to seal. Cut four small slits from the tops of the pies.
5. Spray on the basket of an air fryer with cooking spray. Brush the tops of two tbsp with grape seed oil and then move pies into the air fryer basket using a spatula.
6. Insert jar and then place the temperature to 195 degs C. Bake until golden brown, about 8 min. Remove pies in the basket and then repeat with the rest two pies.
7. Mix powdered milk and sugar in a small bowl. Brush glaze on hot pies and let to dry. Drink pops warm or at room temperature.

Nutrition: Calories 233; Net Carbs 1.3g; Fat 23g; Protein 4.4g;

Muffins with blueberries

Prep T: 25 min | Cook T: 15 min | Servings: 3
Ingredients

- 60 grams of butter
- 60 ml of fresh whole milk
- 140 grams of flour type "00"
- 60 grams of sugar
- 1 egg

- 5 grams of baking powder
- 1/2 sachet of vanillin
- 70 grams of blueberries
- 1/4 tsp of baking soda
- 1 pinch of salt

Cooking tools:

- Baking cups for muffins

Directions

1. Soften the butter at room temperature in the bowl. Add the sugar and then whisk vigorously until a creamy mixture is obtained.
2. Add the egg while continuing to whip.
3. Pour the milk at room temperature slowly, whipping until smooth.
4. Sift the flour into a bowl and mix it together with the baking powder, baking soda, vanillin, and salt. Add them little by little to the mixture until it is creamy and without lumps.
5. Add the blueberries to the dough.
6. Preheat the air fryer to 185 degs C.
7. Fill the baking cups with the mixture.
8. Put the cups with the dough in the basket and insert them into the air fryer.
9. Set the timer to 15 min and bake the muffins until lightly browned.

Nutrition: Calories 287; Fat 3 g; Carbohydrates 2 g; Sugar 3 g; Protein 11 g; Cholesterol 0 mg;

Air Fryer Churros

Prep T: 8 min | Cook T: 15 min |Serving: 4
Ingredients

- 32 grams butter
- 64 grams milk
- 1 pinch salt
- 64 grams flour
- 2 eggs
- 32 grams white sugar
- 1/2 tsp ground cinnamon

Directions

1. Place a saucepan over medium-high heat and melt the butter and once melted add milk and salt. Decrease the heat and while continuing to stir bring to a boil. Instantly add flour all at one time. Keep mixing until the dough comes together.
2. Remove from heat and let cool for 5 to 7 min. Mix in eggs together with the wooden spoon till choux pastry comes together. Spoon dough to a pastry bag fitted with a large star tip—pipe dough into pieces directly into the air fryer bowl.
3. Air fry churros in 175 degs C for 5 min.
4. Meanwhile, blend sugar and cinnamon in a small bowl and then pour on a shallow plate.
5. Eliminate fried churros from the air fryer and roll from the cinnamon-sugar mix.

Nutrition: Calories: 81; Protein: 2g; Fiber: 3g; Net Carbohydrates: 6g;

Tuscan Cantucci

Prep T: 20 min | Cook T: 15 min | Servings: 10
Ingredients

- 250 grams of flour

- 150 grams of coarsely chopped almonds
- 150 grams of sugar
- 50 grams of soft butter
- 2 eggs
- 8 grams of baking powder
- 1/2 glass of white wine

Directions

1. In the mixer or by hand, combine the butter and sugar. Add the yeast and almonds. In two or three times, add the flour, taking care to mix well. Combine the wine several times to obtain a dough from which to obtain a roll of about 7.5 cm in diameter. Cut slices from the roll about 11 mm thick. Arrange on baking paper.
2. Preheat the air fryer to 180 degs C.
3. Place the paper in the basket and insert it into the fryer. Cook for 8-10 min. Turn the cookies over to the other side and bake another 5 min until golden brown.
4. Traditionally they are dipped in sweet wine.

Nutrition: Calories 242; Fat 6.3 g; Carbohydrates 35.5 g; Sugar 17.8 g; Protein 14.8 g; Fiber 2.7g;

Sicilian orange and ricotta cake

Prep T: 20 min | Cook T: 45 min | Servings: 6

Ingredients

- 260 grams of flour
- 250 grams of ricotta
- 3 eggs
- 150 grams of sugar
- 80 grams of sunflower oil
- 10 grams of vanilla yeast for cakes
- 2 grams of salt
- grated peel of an orange
- 20 cm diameter cake pan

Directions

1. In a planetary mixer or with an electric whisk, whip eggs, sugar, and salt. When it reaches a frothy consistency, add the oil and then the ricotta, always whipping. Finally, incorporate the flour, yeast, and orange peel.
2. Preheat the air fryer to 185 degs C. Pour the mixture into the greased and floured pan and cook for about 40-45 min, taking care to open the basket slightly after 30 min to let the humidity escape. Repeat the opening again after 5 min.
3. Rest in the fridge for 2 hours and serve it cold with fresh forest fruit or a sweet orange salad.

Nutrition: Calories 209; Fat 10 g; Carbohydrates 2 g; Sugar 0 g; Protein 40 g; Cholesterol 0 mg;

Strawberry Cake

Prep T: 10 minutes | Cook T: 35 minutes | Servings: 6

Ingredients

- 453 grams of strawberries, chopped
- 128 grams cream cheese, soft
- 32 grams swerve
- 1 tbsp lime juice
- 1 egg, whisked
- 1 tsp vanilla extract
- 3 tbsp coconut oil, melted
- 128 grams almond flour
- 2 tsps baking powder

Directions

1. In a bowl, mix all the ingredients, stir well and pour this into a cake pan lined with parchment paper.
2. Put the pan in the air fryer, cook at 176 degs C for 35 minutes, cool down, slice and serve.

Nutrition: Calories: 200; Fat: 6g; Fiber: 2g; Carbs: 4g; Protein:6g

Strawberry Ricotta Waffles

Prep /Cook T: 20 min. | Servings: 6

Ingredients

- 256 grams flour
- 1 tsp. baking soda, 2tsp baking powder
- 2 eggs
- 2 tbsp. sugar
- 1/2 tsp. vanilla extract
- 256 grams milk
- 32 grams oil
- 64 grams strawberries, sliced
- 32 grams ricotta cheese
- 2 tsp. maple syrup

Directions

1. Preheat the Air Fryer to 200 degs C
2. Whisk the dry and wet batter ingredients.
3. Pour batter into the mold and bake it for 12-15 min.
4. Mix ricotta and vanilla in a bowl. Top with the mixture, syrup, and strawberries.

Nutrition: Calories: 258, Carbs: 37 g, Protein: 16 g, Fat: 5.3 g; Fiber: 4.6; Sugar: 7

Peach and Blueberry Tart

Prep T: 10 min | Cook T: 30 min | Servings: 6 to 8

Ingredients

- 4 peaches, pitted and sliced
- 128 grams fresh blueberries
- 2 tbsp cornstarch
- 3 tbsp sugar
- 1 tbsp freshly squeezed lemon juice
- Cooking Spray
- 1 sheet frozen puff pastry, thawed
- 1 tbsp nonfat or low-fat milk
- Confectioners' sugar, for dusting

Directions

1. Add the blueberries, peaches, sugar, cornstarch, and lemon juice to a large bowl and toss to coat.
2. Spritz a round baking pan with cooking spray.
3. Unfold the pastry and put on the prepared baking pan.
4. Lay the peach slices on the pan, slightly overlapping them. Scatter the blueberries over the peach.
5. Drape the pastry over the outside of the fruit and press pleats firmly together. Brush the milk over the pastry.
6. Place the pan on the bake position.
7. Select Bake, set temperature to 205 degs C, and set time to 30 min.
8. Bake until the crust is golden brown color and the fruit is bubbling.
9. When cooking is complete, remove the pan from the air fryer grill and allow to cool for 10 min.
10. Serve the tart with the confectioners' sugar sprinkled on top.

Nutrition: Calories 223; Fat 12 g; Carbohydrates 27 g; Protein 3 g; Fiber 1.7 g; Sugar 9 g;

Fluffy Italian cappuccino cupcakes

Prep T: 20 min | Cook T: 15 min | Servings: 4

Ingredients

- 100 grams of flour
- 75 grams of olive oil
- 100 grams of sugar
- 1 egg + 1 yolk
- 5 grams of baking powder
- 100 grams of 70% bitter chocolate flakes
- 1 tsp of ground coffee
- Vanilla.
- Muffin cups

Directions

1. In a planetary mixer or with an electric whisk, whip the eggs with the sugar. Sift the flour, yeast, and coffee and add to the dough. In 2 or 3 times, mix the oil and finally add the chocolate flakes.
2. Preheat the air fryer to 185 degs C.
3. Insert the dough into the cups and cook, reducing the temperature to 160 degs C for 12-15 min depending on the size of the cups.
4. Cool and serve.

Nutrition: Calories 154; Fat 1 g; Carbohydrates 13 g; Sugar 8 g; Protein 11 g; Cholesterol 0 mg;

Ricotta And Chocolate Cake

Prep T: 20 min | Cook T: 22 min | Servings: 4

Ingredients

- 2 eggs
- 200 grams of flour

- 100 grams of sugar
- 200 grams of ricotta
- 30 ml of sunflower oil
- 80 grams of chocolate chips
- 10 grams of baking powder
- 20 cm donut pan

Directions

1. Whip eggs and sugar in a planetary mixer. When they are foamy, add the oil and then the ricotta at low speed. Add the flour and baking powder sifted a little at a time to the mixture.
2. Finally, add the chocolate chips. Grease and flour the pan and pour the mixture.
3. Preheat the air fryer at 160 degs C. Cook for 20-22 min. Times may vary according to the size of the mold or the model of the air fryer.

Nutrition: Calories 231; Fat 5 g; Carbohydrates 12 g; Sugar 2 g; Protein 5 g; Cholesterol 0 mg;

Golden Bananas with Chocolate Sauce

Prep T: 10 min | Cook T: 7 min | Servings: 6

Ingredients

- 32 grams cornstarch
- 32 grams plain bread crumbs
- 1 large egg, beaten
- 3 bananas, halved crosswise
- Cooking Spray
- Chocolate sauce, for serving

Directions

1. Place the bread crumbs, egg, and cornstarch in three separate bowls.
2. Roll the bananas in the cornstarch, then in the beaten egg, and finally in the bread crumbs to coat well.
3. Spritz the air fry basket with cooking spray.
4. Arrange the banana halves in the air fry basket and mist them with cooking spray.
5. Place the basket on the air fry position.
6. Select Air Fry, set temperature to 180 degs C, and set time to 7 min.
7. After about 5 min, flip the bananas and continue to air fry for another 2 min.

8. When cooking is complete, remove the bananas from the air fryer grill to a serving plate. Serve now with the chocolate sauce drizzled over the top.

Nutrition: Calories 142; Fat 1.2 g; Carbohydrates 32 g; Protein 2.5 g; Fiber 3 g; Sugar 14 g;

Fast Chocolate Cheesecake

Prep T: 5 min | Cook T: 18 min | Servings: 6

Ingredients

Crust:

- 64 grams butter, melted
- 64 grams coconut flour
- 2 tbsp stevia
- Cooking Spray

Topping:

- 113 grams of unsweetened baker's chocolate
- 128 grams mascarpone cheese, at room temperature
- 1 tsp vanilla extract
- 2 drops peppermint extract

Directions

1. Lightly coat a pan with some cooking spray.
2. In a bowl, mix together the flour, butter, and stevia until well combined. Transfer the mixture to the baking pan.
3. Place the pan on the bake position.
4. Select Bake, set temperature to 180 degs C, and set time to 18 min.
5. When done, a toothpick inserted in the center should come out of it clean.
6. Remove the crust from the air fryer grill to a wire rack to cool.
7. Once cooled completely, place it in the freezer for 20 min.
8. When ready, combine all the ingredients for the topping in a small bowl and stir to incorporate.
9. Spread this topping over the crust and let it sit for another 15 min in the freezer.
10. Serve chilled.

Nutrition: Calories 177; Fat 14 g; Carbohydrates 6.4 g; Protein 6.4 g; Fiber 2.7 g; Sugar 1 g;

Chocolate Soufflé for Two

Prep T: 5 min | Cook T: 14 min |Serving: 2

Ingredients

- 2 tbsp. Almond flour
- 1/2 tsp. vanilla
- 3 tbsp. sweetener
- 2 separated eggs
- 32 grams melted coconut oil
- 85 grams of semi-sweet chocolate, chopped

Directions

1. Brush coconut oil and sweetener onto ramekins.
2. Melt coconut oil and chocolate together.
3. Beat egg yolks well, adding vanilla and sweetener. Stir in flour and ensure there are no lumps.
4. Preheat the air fryer oven to 165 degs C.
5. Whisk egg whites till they reach peak state and fold them into chocolate mixture.
6. Pour batter into ramekins and place them into the air fryer oven.
7. Cook 14 min.
8. Serve with powdered sugar dusted on top.

Nutrition: Calories: 238; Fat: 6g; Protein: 1g; Sugar: 4g;

Index

Z

Manufactured by Amazon.ca
Bolton, ON

26377595R00044